THE SAME MOON SHINES

ON US ALL

Poems 2004 - 2015

Harald Wyndham

THE SAME MOON SHINES ON US ALL, Poems 2004 - 2015, by Harald Wyndham, is published by Blue Scarab Press on November 1st, 2015. Edition limited to 300 copies.

ISBN 978-0-937179-19-2

THE SAME MOON SHINES ON US ALL was manufactured by Litho Printing, Pocatello, Idaho.

Cover artwork by Linda Wolfe, Idaho Rostered Artist, winner of the Governor's Award. Aside from publication here, Linda Wolfe retains all rights to the painting.

Photograph of Harald Wyndham by Sierra Diane Wyndham, 2015

Blue Scarab Press acknowledges with thanks the prior publication of some of these poems in the following periodicals or special editions:

Pocatello Arts Council Literary Pavers: *The Treasuries of the Snow*

I Ask the Stars to Bring Me Home Again, 2007, Limberlost Press, Boise, Idaho. Complete text included in section seven, *Climbing Mount Bonneville*.

Our Voices, 2003, Ronald Snake Edmo, for poem *Climbing Mount Bonneville*.

The Struggle, Blue Scarab Press, 2011. All of the poems in section five, *Prayers From the Fire*, are from this previously published collection. Also, the poem, *Lent*, in section four, *The Birds of God*.

THE SAME MOON SHINES ON US ALL contains the occasional use of adult concepts and language. Some poems may not be appropriate for children.

Address all correspondence to Blue Scarab Press, P.O. Box 4966, Pocatello, Idaho 83205 or email haraldwyndham@gmail.com.

THE SAME MOON SHINES ON US ALL

I am sixty-nine this year. Amazing thought. Some mornings I feel sixteen; others, more like eighty. The body and I often have different agendas. At some point, in the not too distant future, we will part company. Meanwhile, as long as possible, we go on long walks or sit on the front steps and look at the rising moon. Sometimes, as we do those things, poems arise.

This is my fourth collection of poems gleaned from a decade of days, the back corners of years, from misguided inspirations, gifts of the Muse, rants and raves, late night cups of coffee and jaundiced looks in the mirror. Some poems reflect dark times -- world-wide conflict, war and unspeakable atrocity -- days spent in solitude with my arms wrapped round my knees. But more have come from days redeemed by sunlight and nights of the full moon, who rises monthly to look me in the face.

The moon is the dominant image for this collection. The book's title, and that of its first section, come from a lovely, rollicking poem about children all over the world, connected to each other by looking at the same moon. Linda Wolfe's exceptional painting for the cover expresses the magic and energy discovered by children encountering the moon. There is still hope for mankind in their perpetual willingness to be amazed.

The book has seven sections, rather like an orchestral piece. Some sections are *andante cantabile*, set to a walking tune. Others are *allegreto, lento, con brio, scherzo* and *furioso*. There are repetitive leitmotifs of moon and marriage, birds and small towns, that stitch the sections together, as well as broader themes of faith-struggles, war-struggles and wide open country that you can either travel through or skip over as you choose. Hopefully, in one or more of the sections is a poem to make you laugh or smile or pause with a glimmering eye. That's how I felt when they first showed up at my door. Scattered throughout, in loose knots of formal interludes or courtly dances, are a plethora of sonnets, spun out of moonbeams and marigolds.

The moon is our ultimate Muse, since time immemorial. Endlessly fascinating, eternally beckoning, she feeds our moods, be they joyful or sorrowing, and shares our solitary dramas without judging, but perhaps fostering hope. As this book goes to press, I think of the vast streams of refugees from the Syrian wars in their desperate journey across Europe, sleeping for better or worse with the moon for a blanket. If she can bring some comfort to them then we can say with conviction that line from Midsummer Night's Dream -- "Well shone, Moon."

Wherever you find yourself next time the moon catches your attention, take a moment to step away from the urgency of the moment and think of all the faces it is shining on.

Harald Wyndham

Thus, in spite of our wretchedness --
because we think
and are so aware of our lives
in the face of infinity --
we have the advantage
over the Universe that dwarfs us
with its infinite space and depth and incomprehensibility.

    -- Blaise Pascal

From LOVE AND MARRIAGE, A Sonnet Cycle, 1973

On warm September nights, I drive the car
Out to the dry meadows to walk under the stars.
They stare down from the dark blue vault of heaven,
Dwarfing my sorrows beneath their colossal patterns.
To know my body is less than a sliver of grass,
Glued to a speck of macrocosmic dust,
Mocks self-pity and puts pride in its place.
With terror and awe I lift my hands into space,
Asking nothing, unable to utter a prayer,
Offering my life to the vast Lord who is everywhere,
Invisible, unnameable, ruler of light and dark,
In whom I move and breathe, for whom I work
On love's behalf, struggling to build and protect
The shimmering variations of infinite, unfathomable Intellect.

THE SAME MOON SHINES

ON US ALL

THE SAME MOON SHINES ON US ALL

The children from Delhi dance in blue silk
    chanting their sinuous songs,
while the kids from the Congo beat on big drums,
    and the same moon shines on us all.

The children from Moscow ride sleds in the snow
    where icicles hang from the trees,
while the kids from Bahrain trace designs in the sand,
    and the same moon shines on us all.

The children from Omaha carve pumpkins at night
    with candles to make their eyes glow,
while the kids from Osaka fly dragon-tailed kites,
    and the same moon shines on us all.

The children from Stockholm sing songs of the sea,
    wearing costumes embroidered in blue,
while the kids from Rangoon dance in crimson and gold,
    and the same moon shines on us all.

The children from Beijing write poems on scrolls
    beneath lanterns of purple and green,
while the kids from La Paz dig potatoes and dance,
    and the same moon shines on us all.

The children from Brooklyn play tag in the streets,
    dodging the trucks and the cars,
while the kids from Tikrit sit on rooftops and sing,
    and the same moon shines on us all.

The children from Gaza tell stories all night
    about peace in a far-away land,
while the kids from Netanya build fires on the beach,
    and the same moon shines on us all.

The children from Paris and London and Split,
    from Toronto, Buenos Aires, Mumbai,
from Cape Town and Cairo, Cancun and Hanoi
    from Belgrade, Helsinki , Shanghai,
from Naples and Athens, Tehran and New York,
    from Chicago, Berlin and Saint Paul,
Dream their big wishes and dance their bright songs,
    and the same moon shines on us all.

BLUE MOON AT THE END OF THE STREET

I see her through the open door in passing,

Go outside and sit on the front steps,

Late July, tree branches stirring gently overhead,

Cool enough for a light jacket, warm enough for shorts,

Like a full bowl of cream hanging there

Above the dark trees, at the end of the street,

The air alive with cat-calls and traffic noises

As if I were fourteen again, itchy, in love,

The moment a held breath, glassy water,

Unbroken by intrusion of another,

Attention focused on her face completely

Moving leaf by leaf into the clear,

Nothing between us now but vibrant air,

And I have all I need just being here.

IT IS BY POEMS THAT WE LIVE

It is by poems that we live
                and keep alive

               that within us which otherwise
the world and life would
            break,
               kill,
                  mock,
                     destroy

or shape into the common mask
               that all must wear

               except
    in secret

where
    like unfurled banners of unrepentant

            JOY!

      we dance!

            and sing!

  and laugh!

          and are redeemed.

THE EAGERNESS WITHIN

Each Wednesday I give a little water to
the three kalanchoe, orange and red,
in their small pots on the south windowsill.

It seems stingy, but is in fact sufficient.
To be generous is to drown them.
And look at the results!

They yearn and stretch
and climb the window glass
with segments limber as dancer's arms

and fingers filled with blossoms,
'til the weight of their appetite
for sunlight nearly topples them.

I love their raw desire -- so like mine! --
reaching from dry ground to the light divine.

MOTHER'S THINGS

All Saint's Day.

I get out your wooden sewing box from Bavaria.
The sides are a bit warped
and painted flowers faded from years on the windowsill.
Your birthday today.
Had you lived, you would be eighty-five.
Inside, a thimble, darning-sock, Boy Scout patches, thread,
some metal buttons from a uniform.

I keep forgetting how long you have been dead.

I also have your leather purse with a brass snap.
Inside, a pocketbook and driver's license.
No money. A few
black and white photographs
from Germany.
A Certificate of Naturalization dated
January 23, 1952.
An embroidered handkerchief --
perhaps your mother's.
A few dried tears.

Your old world proverbs stick in my brain still:
"I'd like to be unhappy, but I never have the time."

Some costume jewelry
in the music box with its painting
of the Matterhorn,
that played 'Clair de Lune'
until I over-wound it one afternoon.
Mother-of-pearl broach and
a gaudy stick-pin with green and blue glass beads.
Your delicate gold wrist watch
with the broken stem.

Where are you now?
The violin sonatas of Johann Sebastian Bach
surround me in this room.

All Saints Day.
So close.
So far away.

EAST OF MISSOULA

Wraiths of mist
rise off the Clark Fork
east of Missoula,
the sky brightening
so that the aspens appear as
dark gold witnesses
beside the river
and small farmhouses
at the mouths of steep canyons,
the kitchen lights already on
as people begin their day.

What a country this is.

What a damned beautiful country this is.

THE SOURCE

The deep ravine, furrowed
    By running water,
        Covered by long strands
    Of field grass.

I want to climb down,
    Sit in the dark cleft,
        Huddle, hunch,
    And be held there.

What man am I to want?
    What boy? What child?
        So moved to this raw place,
    Alone, and wild.

I am my mother's son,
    My wife's husband.
        One foot in the grave,
    My heart in her hand.

THE EIGHTEENTH OF MARCH

Winter's last snowfall without wind,
By morning, inch deep on the power-lines,
Filling the needles of the evergreen,
Topping fence-posts and rails.

In the aspen grove
Bits and clumps dust out of branches
As a hawk lifts off with a *scree!*
Otherwise stillness fills the fields,
No footprints on the road but mine.

    It is the fifth year of the war.

The elaborate branches of the sage brush
Sport tiny seed plumes, delicately
Tufted with snow.
Willow stems, dark red by the stream,
Water noises under drifts
In the ravine,
And here, a broken nest,
Half-filled with snowflakes.

    Refuge, refuge, o battered soul.

SLEEPWORK

Grains of grief
    slip through the seams of sleep

They need to be gathered
    into a soft sock
    at the edge of dreaming

Lost souls abandoned without thinking

Failures in love, injuries, bruises unhealed

Chances missed or misunderstood
    stand at bedside in the quiet room

We sort and gather with fingertips,
    digging into corners,
    seeking out lost names

        rice grains
        sand grains
        slippery smooth
        rough edged

They catch our breath
    scratch the eye's corner
    worry into tight, dark places
    just beyond reach

We toss and turn,
    they shift from side to side

Companions, night watchers,
    uncounted beads of fate

Our fingers polish their faces

    too late

    too late

JANE, PLAYING PIANO AFTER DINNER

She is playing Schubert
On the small, upright piano
In this grand house she designed in the mountains,
Practicing a skill learned long ago
When she was a small girl in her parent's home
On the farm in Ohio, years before
We met and married, before
The long wars and struggles of our generation.
Nine presidents ago she was playing,
Before we knew each other, when I was a young boy
Passing newspapers in that little town
With no idea she lived six miles to the south.
The Schubert rendered carefully,
Feeling her way once more through the notes,
Pausing imperceptibly to read a bar
That is in shadow, correcting a natural to a flat,
Playing cross-hand in some spots, on this
Mild September evening after dinner, as the sun
Melts all over the horizon, crimson and gold,
Splaying the walls of the living room,
And I lie on the sofa, listening to her play,
Drawn once more into childhood,
Our parents alive again,
The world at peace,
The future
Something we couldn't even imagine.

FORTY-FIRST ANNIVERSARY

Sometimes when I think of our first years
They seem so far away as if we had lived
Across oceans of time and space in a world
Of old photo albums and brown faces,
Cornfields, small towns, young children . . .
The anxious yearning of those distant days,
Wondering where life would lead and whether
We could make a place for ourselves in the world,
Is overwhelming when I think what we dared and did.
Looking back, I see now what I could not see --
How fine you were, how beautiful and true,
And how careless a companion I was to you.
Your patient, faithful love amazes me
Much more today than on the day we married.

MOTHER MOON

The full moon after midnight
Ices the hayfield fence.
I stare at it entranced,
Waking to use the toilet.
Later, at six, driving to work
It is lambent and brassy
Above the purple knife-edge
Of the western ridge,
Yellow as a prayer wheel,
A seasoned, benevolent friend
To the first birds cutting the sky
Above the valley green as a lost Eden.

Great mother, Diana, Astarte, eternal courtesan,
Bless this lover as he wanders out into the world.

HAVING TEA WITH FATHER

'High tea,' you called it, only half joking.
'Very British, you know,' assuming a
Bloomsbury accent, assuming character
From your lost father, who was English,
And that long lineage back to William of
Normandy, castles in Cockermouth, Earls
And the rest of it, which, on leave in World
War Two, you visited to have tea with
A great uncle Percy, and which your namesake
Continues to explore, searching restlessly
Through genealogies for each blood-line.

I, who share no blood, only parenting,
Sense you strong at the table tonight,
(Though you now are many years gone)
Drink my solitary tea in the October dark
And stare at my white beard in the window glass.
Although I quit smoking decades ago
I hungrily smell one of those freshly-lit
Phillip Morris straights we shared
In the kitchen after Mother died,
Your eyes a little watery, from the smoke.

There is no need to say anything.
Never was. We sat there like two men,
Veterans of the life wars, marriage,
Home repairs, mortgage, personal griefs,
And drank our cups of *Orange Pekoe* tea --
Yours straight, mine with too much sugar --
Asking from time to time innocuous questions
About weather or the recent gossip in town.
Never touching the unspoken depths of love
Or death or where the pain comes from.
We savored each other's company.

And so tonight -- thanks, Dad, for dropping by.
I think about you more than you would guess.
Hope you like the tea I drink these days --
Earl Grey, imported directly from England.
'Very British, you know.'

THE FULL MOON IN HER MAJESTY ARISES

The full moon in her majesty arises
over the ridgeline, flooding the fields with silver,
glimmering the patio stones, my knees and hands.
I sit on the wooden bench in a veil of silence,
this quiet, warm, cloudless September night.

How often have we stared thus at each other?
Sixty years at least, with the same pure longing.
I join your many paramours around the world,
amazed to have been alive so long,
so often in your presence over the years.

My old companion, solace and true friend,
giver of passive confidence, remover of fear.
We stare at each other an hour, the moon and I.
Asking nothing. Giving no reply.

A FEW DAYS BEFORE EQUINOX

Spring dawn light.

Fresh snowfall frosts the ridgeline trees.

The eastern horizon swept clean of stars
    save one the Magi saw --
                  bright Jupiter --
    a silver torch above the mountain's edge.

I stand in the dark room, naked, at the window.

The tiny point of a satellite crosses the sky.

Below, dark meadows, snow-banks nearly gone.

We greet each other, Jupiter and I.

IN THE ENGLISH GARDENS

Leaves overlapping leaves
Overlapping years, poems, dreams.
Bright October morning with hoarfrost
Sugaring the unmowed grass and empty benches
As I scuff the leaf-strewn gravel lanes
Leaving the first wet footprints of the day.

Pathways overlap and cross
Beneath disheveled trees,
Discarding gold and scarlet shards
On the mound of the Monopteros.
The channels of the Isar cross
Through meadow and wooded lanes
Leading one to amble aimlessly
In ice cold morning sun
With memory, that wandering dog, unleashed.

At any moment I could meet someone --
My mother riding on her bicycle,
Or Oma walking with her dackle hound,
Grandpa with his paper and cigar
Strolling to the Chinese Tower to have a beer.
I could meet myself a quarter century ago
Hobbling along with my sore knee,
Or the mystery lady I was searching for
Surprising me with a smile --
Bright eyes beneath black hair --
Before vanishing like laughter into the air.

Instead, I am accompanied
By two companions, one on either arm,
Visible from the corner of each eye --
The boy in shorts, who is my soul, on the right --
The skeletal, hooded shadow on the left.
Together we cross the open space
Where on the green horizon of the town,
As on a postage stamp, arise the double domes
Of the lady church, telling me no matter where I go
In this wide world, Munich is my home.

POLAND, AUGUST 31, 1939

The normal busyness of everyone walks sweetly by . . .
Birds in the branches, sun in the sky, lovers hand in hand . . .

The afternoon golden and evening warm and dry,
A coffee on the boulevard outside your favorite café,
Chit-chat, worries over this and that, despair
Over a sweetheart, woman or man, who is not there.

One has one's set position and knows one's place,
Nods or tips one's hat to the passerby, gentile or Jew,
Wanders the tree-lined boulevard, then turns
To climb the stairwell to a lover's room . . .

Sunset gilds the fairy castle cloudbanks.
Cigar smoke drifts in the air, with a whiff of diesel.
A distant tremor makes the tea-cups tremble.

Across the border, Panzers form their ranks.

THE YELLOW TREE

leaves half-stripped
        by wind and rain
still dignified
        in tattered glory
shreds of soft gold
        scattered over stark limbs

I see myself in you
        yellow tree

I see myself
        in you

FOR THE DEAD AT SANDY HOOK

Eternal things are all we hold in mind
in a world unmade by murder at the school --
the temporal things we seek cannot be found.

Birds that flicker brightly branch to branch,
smooth stones glistening in the broken stream,
become the names we say without a sound.

Dawn Hochsprung, Mary Sherlach, Anne Marie Murphy,
who sprang with sudden courage toward the guns.
Victoria Soto, Lauren Gabrielle Rousseau, Rachel D'Avino
who shielded with their bodies the innocent ones.

And those children -- clear faces, bright eyes, smiles --
all natural things -- blue sky, bird flight, waterfall --
become the permanent treasury of their names:

Charlotte, Daniel, Olivia, Josephine and Ana,
Dylan, Madeleine, Catherine, Chase and Jesse,
James, Grace, Emilie, Jack and Noah,
Caroline, Jessica, Avielle, Benjamin, Allison.

And *Nancy*, mother, murdered by her son,
his name held back, unspeakable, unspoken.

On all these names cry mercy, every one.
Cry mercy on our hearts and voices broken.

WALKING AT NOON UNDER THE TREES

At noon, today, I walk shaded lanes of the cemetery
as is my habit when the weather is hot. Within three steps
I enter the boundless realms of unrestricted thought,
one idea folding over another, as my feet follow each other
without being taught. I read the names on the stones,
the dates of their lives and deaths decades ago,
and think of my own parents, neighbors and friends
in that small Ohio town, their faces rising up like lotus flowers
from the darkness I carry within, that 'kelson of creation,'
trembling on the surface before re-submerging into
tree shadow and the intensely green grass, alive and wet.
It may be that we do not survive our bodies,
but are gone, diffused in luminescent water and earth and air,
and that this composition of walking chemistry that is myself will be
dissolved and scattered, re-mixed, recombined into new things,
but never have the same heart, mind, spirit, body and soul ever again.
And I am at peace with that, hoping little else for heaven
except someone for a moment hold onto a fragment of
my face, my voice, a poem, song or kindness, before
letting go and allowing the dross to sink to the common darkness
with all the others, my name and dates on a stone
boasting their quaint and useless facts to the birds and the rain.

I have no less to lose, no more to gain.

ANOTHER BROKEN SHELL

ALONG THE BEACH

ANOTHER BROKEN SHELL ALONG THE BEACH

A winter's morning walk along the gulf,
miles of white sand far as the eye can see,
and moderate surf from last night's storm beating the shore;
I saunter along the edge, where the sand is wet
in blue-jeans, jacket and hat, old tennis shoes,
haphazard, absently, transfixed by the debris
each wave brings in with a foaming roar, and find
another broken shell along the beach.

This one is almost perfect, curved on itself,
the curled top partly crushed, the orange whorl
pitted by wear and chipped on the edges, yet shiny
with a lacquer of gunmetal gray where the creature retracted
its glistening body to secure inner chambers now
long since abandoned, compacted with sand, forlorn,
the hollow relic of a vanished living being . . .
another broken shell along the beach.

It joins the others jostling in my pockets,
those found worthy for being curious, odd colored, nearly perfect,
standing out from the listless scrum of broken shells the wave foam stirs,
a charnel house of eyeless skulls, amphora, clams, bones, feathers, detritus
picked over by sandpipers and the occasional seagull, like shoppers
at a bargain discount store, where broken things, shelved in strata,
slowly disintegrate, nameless, faceless, forgotten, dead . . .
another broken shell along the beach.

What do we leave behind us when we die?
Houses of disembodied artifacts, books, furniture and photographs,
faces no one remembers, paintings, shirts, shoes, cooking pots, arrowheads,
indecipherable scripts, jokes, legends elaborated into myths by our progeny,
touchstones of memory -- mother's hand on my head as her scissors snipped,
her music box and Bavarian proverbs; father's pipe-smoke and love of dogs,
his workbench smelling of sawdust, a paint-smeared knife . . .
another broken shell along the beach.

Not even the greatest names of the human race leave more.
Buddha, Jesus, Homer, Dante, Shakespeare, Galileo, Newton, Bach,
Beethoven, Einstein, his equations on a chalkboard, leave their joyous dancing,
insights, intricate thoughts, music, logical theorems, science, plays and poetry
like elaborate sculptured shells to be lifted up, while of the once-living personality
we know only fragments and rumors, uncertain records, forgeries, the mystery
vanished forever -- "Alas, poor Yorick, I knew him, Horatio" . . .
another broken shell along the beach.

The great collective efforts of mankind, pyramids, the Great Wall,
mounds of the dawn people, henges of stacked stone, Easter Island statues,
Machu Picchu, Parthenon, pillars of Persepolis, Petra and the coliseum in Rome,
Temple of Jerusalem, cathedrals, aqueducts, the library at Alexandria,
modern cities as well, Paris, London, New York, Washington, Hong Kong,
hanging gardens, canals, skyscrapers, boot-prints of the first man on the moon --
"My name is Ozymandias, king of kings: Look on my works ye Mighty and despair" . . .
another broken shell along the beach.

It is easy to despair. What will remain of this small life?
Thoughts scribbled in notebooks, some articles, some poems
buried so deep in the strata they scarce exist, incommunicable, invisible.
What can I create that would do you good? What do you need to hear?
The energy, the music, the shouting and dance, the gleaming brain
secure in its dark chamber, fiddling furiously on an empty stage . . .
"I have heard the mermaids singing, each to each" . . .
another broken shell along the beach.

What of it? We are solitary souls, enigmatic, inscrutable, alive.
For all my tireless ambitions, twists of grief, confronting futility and the
unceasing crash of wave upon wave casting up shells to mock my arrogant
pretensions of immortality, in private morning solitude with irreverent exuberance,
standing on tiptoe to salute infinity, laughing, leaping, dancing in my soul,
my voice defiant, drowned in the slap of relentless surf, shouts out
Lord Byron's line: "Roll on, thou deep and dark blue Ocean, -- roll!" . . .
another broken shell along the beach.

REQUIEM FOR THE PEOPLE OF AI

When Israel had finished killing all the inhabitants of Ai in the open ground and where they followed them into the wilderness, and when all to a man had fallen by edge of the sword, all Israel returned to Ai and slaughtered all its people. The number who fell that day, men and women together, was twelve thousand, all people of Ai.

Joshua, Chapter 8

Weep for the people of Ai,
marginal farmers, small city dwellers,
shopkeepers, school teachers, mothers and fathers,
mud bricks and insubstantial walls,
nothing of value, out of date weapons,
defenses neglected, subsistence economy,
no advocates with power, no friends to speak of,
no one to care if they live or they die,
easy targets for target practice,
put to the sword, spear, machine gun, machete, RPG,
hand-grenade, helicopter, Lt. Calley's lighter
or the fifteen year old son of a mayor,
shot for a thrill by soldiers bored by their victories,
body counts, always counting the bodies,
holy statistics, justifying something
or nothing at all -- what matter?
They're not even human, these
people of Ai, just in the way, an obstacle
to remove to make room for some condo's or
palace, a temple, a bank, an eighteen-hole golf course,
their small tools, statues, pictures and trinkets
demolished with houses and burned with the trash.
These non-people, nameless, sand-niggers, rag-heads,
husbands and wives, small children, folks of no consequence,
caught on the wrong side, trusting the wrong gods,
'collateral damage', forgotten, forgettable,
running like sheep before the righteous guns.

Oh, pray for their souls, weep for their lives,
who were human, like you and me -- these people of Ai.

NOCTURNE, SUMMER SOLSTICE, 2012

Midnight on the patio, shorts and a t-shirt.

                                                    Freedom.

The moon, three-quarters full in the southern sky.

To the east, on the dark ridge-line,
            amber squares of distant windows glow.
                        Overhead, just visible in moonlight, a few bright stars.

There is no sound at all --
            no bark, no traffic noise, no trains, no wind-stirred leaves, no insect chirp.
            The atmosphere is holding its breath.

                        rush of blood in my ears hammers on silence

The world (the Universe), so filled with noise, violence and exploding stars,
            wars, arguments, parades, accidents, singing and fiery death,
                        withdraws its claim on this particular moment.

I am
            infinitely surrounded
                        by what I apprehend but cannot name.

                        Hello . . . hello . . .?
                                    Is someone there?

                        Who are you?

                                    (& who,
                                                after all,
                                                            am I?)

PLEASURES OF THE MORNING

Mountain sunrise flares on the snowy fields.
The tiny crystals of ice sparkle like chips of fire.

Sunlight pours into my library, also,
Flaring off the faces of flat books,
Words of men and women just like me
Who took days as they found them --
Sun, cloud, rain, storm and wind -- *Elation!* --
And made a poem, a story, song or psalm,
Like a handprint painted on a cave wall
To last long after the moment of creation,
To say -- 'I am here!' -- knowing that they would
Pass away and be completely forgotten as persons,
Their lives accessible only through their words.

The air is alive with sparks from these great poets,
Sun streaming through dust to warm their dust-jackets,
So they are more pleased perhaps to have words spoken aloud,
Than by honors and prizes the world hands out.
Sparkling syllables flare up everywhere,
Freely as random flakes in the sun-bright fields,
To be grasped this moment only, like a gift
That melts when it is touched, yet still
Reflects its gift of fire to the mind
Open to receive it, as I am,
Who have all the time in the world,
And sit on my knees here, hands spread to the sun,
Tasting their fiery syllables with my tongue.

THE BEES

Even the bees
Are tired of working for us,
Doing our bidding, flying from tree to tree,
Pollinating thousands of acres of crops for free.
Their stacked hives like prison cells race down the freeways
From state to state on semi trucks at night,
The tiny convicts in striped jackets
Hired out on work release.

But the bees are disappearing,
Skipping bail, sawing through bars,
Checking out without
Two weeks notice or filing a grievance
With their attorneys, they just
sneak out after dark,
Leaving the hives empty.

Like polar icecaps and tropical rainforests,
The bees are bidding us good riddance.
They've had enough -- goodbye!
They don't give a damn if we live or die.

AT THE WAILING WALL

What to pray for?

Standing before the massive stones
of Herod's long lost temple
as if at the Ear of God,
I take out notebook and pencil.

There are so many concerns --
my wife and children, my health, my job,
the starving poor, the refugee camps, the wars,
the burning forests, polluted oceans, earthquakes, floods . . .

Surrounded by devoted Sephardim
in black coats and hats, reciting
scripture as they nod their heads,
I scribble one word and shove it into a crack.

Peace.

CROSSING SHANGHAI FERRY

We crowd onto a diesel-fumed commercial ferry boat
On the "new side" of Shanghai, one block away
From the modern, exquisite Shangri-La Hotel,
where vendors of beef-sticks barbequed on bicycle fenders
Offer their wares to the crowd of arriving passengers.
We surge on board, driven by the press of bodies
To crowd the open deck, pushed to the far rails
By pedestrians, bicycles, ancient motorbikes
As the ferry foams away in a sputter of black diesel
And we float out onto the broad river's back
Like a small neon bug crossing a dragon's scales.
Our goal -- the skyline spoked with lighted towers,
Capped with golden lotus flowers and red pyramids
Rising behind the "Bund" neighborhood of the old city.

A passing freighter moans its solemn horn --
on every side the future is being born.

As we approach the glittery dockside, restaurants and bars,
The ferry heels and nuzzles to the wharf. The passengers press
for advantage, their departure a rush down the gangplank,
Into the smudge of streets, narrow alleys, murky market shops,
Racks of ancient bicycles and motor scooters chained up
against the mad weave and honk of aggressive traffic,
Sidewalk vendors of roasted chicken, pancakes, noodles,
Pulse of corpuscles clogging the arteries of this reviving heart.

We stand and let the stream surge by around us.
Then plunge in to wave down a cab to the restaurant.

PASSAGE TO CHINA

We are crossing the Aleutian Islands.

Soon we will fly over
> The International Date Line
> and enter another world.

The world of tomorrow, already up and about,
Where faces and voices are new
> And there is nothing to do
> But face them.

Soon we will be over Vladivostok.

CONSOLATIONS OF LAND AND SKY

Orion strides over the mountain in early evening,
Following the Pleiades down the southern sky.

Autumn equinox, darkness increasing each day.
Frost nips the geraniums and tomato plants.

We are lost in Iraq, mired in permanent war.
The permafrost is melting in Siberia.

No one knows what new catastrophe
Is unfolding even now across the world.

Driving a country road, past river marsh,
I notice cattails swaying yellow and brown.

The bench-land cheat-grass is dry as tinder.
Maples bleed in the crotches of the canyons.

For half an hour I forget about everything.
Then drive home to face the inevitable news.

HIGH WIND ON THE GREAT WALL

The winds continually blow hard and cold
At the watch tower on the Great Wall.
One thousand tourists from all over the world
Climb the uneven stairway up and down,
Navigating steep steps, ridges and ramps,
Holding handrails and each others' arms
To look over battlements at the threaded seam
Of twisted stone stitched onto the ridgelines,
Range after distant range of stark stone mountains,
Flashing with red and yellow maples amid green scrub.

It is October. The flat winds cut through clothing
With the first sharp edge of winter. Somewhere
A mountain or two away, the Mongol hordes
Mounted their tough war horses.
Down below, in the hardscrabble village
Their progeny in colorful slippers and caps
Assault the tourists with "Hello! Hello! Hello!"
pushing t-shirts, brass bells, fans of scarlet and gold
with smudgy hands and faces, shivering despite
their padded jackets in the chill shadows of late afternoon.

The tourists flow through them and only a few are caught
In the web of harangue and hype. Many are wearing
Their best clothing -- formal suits, elegant dresses --
As if going to a wedding or holiday celebration --
Some women wear high heeled shoes -- some
Have brought their aged parents who can barely walk,
And here a legless man pulls himself up by his arms
While a pilgrim crawls along on hands and knees.

I stand by a notch in a watch-tower, surveying the country.
No danger of barbarians today. Just the natives
Making pilgrimage, along with Americans, Australians, Japanese,
Germans, French, Brits and Hindu businessmen,
People with video cameras crawling over everything.
This is what it comes to with these monuments --
Great pyramids, great fortresses, great wall --
Another thing to go take pictures of,
Bring the kids and eat lunch on a high point
Where long ago forgotten people died.

THE EAST WIND

Sweeps over the land unexpected,
making the horses rear up nervously,
bringing strange, dark, dangerous clouds.

Rises in the soul as well , stirring up trouble.
A man leaves wife and family without warning,
runs away with the lady from the hardware store
for a two week torrid affair across state lines.
Armies invade small countries, corporations collapse,
stockbrokers steal billions and flee to Zanzibar.
Governments of flat, mid-western states declare
their independence, presidents resign in disgrace.

> *A smolder in the blood, gleam in the eye,*
> *burn in the saddle, itch in the feet, wanderlust or*
> *just plain lust -- a sea change, the wild East wind*
> *loosening things up that were tied down.*
> *The boom swings wide and the sails fill out.*
> *We wheel about and run before the storm,*
> *hell-bent for Indonesia or Madagascar.*

Later, after it blows over, shame and regret,
returning to ruined cities, homes, lives,
to senses once more tame and rational,
that look on devastation with despair, asking
"How could we, how could I have done it?"
No answer, only to say -- the East wind rose
in my heart and everything suddenly
fell into place -- then fell apart.

ANNIVERSARY, 2004

All day, as I was working at the office,
Hounded by a hundred urgent unimportant distractions,
You thought about me and about our wedding day
Thirty-eight years ago on a bright Saturday morning in June
In the front room parlor of the Reverend Mr. Jepson
In Mt. Victory, Ohio, with our parents and your sister for
Witnesses, you in white silk with your hair pulled back
Above your forehead, me in my formal wool herringboned suit,
Were joined that morning in holy matrimony, bound
Together in five minutes of ceremony by rings that have not yet
Been discarded, exhausted, lost or worn out, despite
The rough and exciting roads we have ridden together,
And so you made a meat loaf for our dinner
As a simple expression of undying love.

THERE IS A GREATNESS IN AMERICA

Rises like blue mist out of the fields,
Like saffron vapor hovering over the river
On a summer morning outside Davenport, Iowa,
Where the wind-blown prairie starts its wild run
Like a strong heart yearning toward horizons,
Escaping the confinement of past lives,
Old histories with their sad accoutrements
Strewn in the wheel-ruts as the independent spirit,
Seeking nothing less than solitude
Strides out boldly toward the scarcely imagined mountains.

A STONE FOR STEVEN P.

So many leave suddenly,
at night, without warning,
an hour of trauma,
EMT's working like ditch diggers
        to save the flailing soul
                sinking in deep waters
and then it is finished
and the other rituals begin --
the coroner, the gurney, papers to sign.

And somewhere, on the thin horizon,
almost out of sight, the small
thin boat sails off
and one lifts a tired hand
to wave, in shock, numbly, not at all ready
to say goodbye.

Later, among the books and photographs,
the piles of papers left behind,
relics, cherished things,
pots and pans once used for spaghetti sauce,
knives and spatulas, colanders, old keys,
things to put in boxes to give away
and finally, the ashes themselves
poured into the outgoing waves of the north Atlantic.

We scarcely understand how little
remains of any life -- that it
only remains in those
who loved and lived with and remember him.

To help us not forget
those bright eyes, gray beard, ponytail, poems and laughter,
we put one stone on the kitchen windowsill.
One tiny,
        simple,
                heartbreakingly heavy stone.

APPALOOSA BODISATTVA BUDDY SKY

Happy birthday, Gino -- may you live forever

When you find your true name, life begins.

Some take hold of the one they were given,
Loving its heritage of patriarchs and cattle thieves,
Others are seeking, listening, watching all night
Till what they have always been rises up
Like a lotus in still water in moonlight
And they reach out to touch it
And know who they are.

Thus Jacob becomes Israel, Saul becomes Paul,
Zimmerman becomes Dylan and one Friedrich Stowasser
Becomes Friedensreich Regentag Dunkelbunt Hundertwassers.
Billy Two-Bears comes back from the desert as Coyote Moon
And Siddartha awakens under the Bo tree as the Buddha.

So too, one nuclear Adam, Buddy "Russet" Clays,
Throwing a football over a spud-cellar into the stars,
Finds in a cosmic soap-bubble blown from a long trombone
The 'Cowboy Buddha,' an Appaloosa rising into the sky
And touches the lotus, tender in moonlight,
His true name -- Bo -- Bodisattva --
Buddy Gino Sky.

CRAZY MAD SAD FIREWORKS FOR BILL

William Vern Studebaker (May 1947 - July 4, 2008)
Drowned on the East Fork of the Salmon near Yellow Pine

The image still too fresh --
    evergreen branches newly cut and fragrant on the floor --
      nothing else intrudes --
    poems, pictures, books, artifacts --
      residue of a full life --
        wait in their back corner
          for a later time, empty and dry.

Today we are filled with the yet still vibrant life --
    pungent, strongly felt, almost
      palpable in this room overflowing with friends --
and there is nothing to be done
      but breathe it deeply in, this life, and hold it fresh and alive
        as long as we can --
          this man we loved, held strong in memory.

His rough brush-top of hair, uncombed and natural --
    the wry twist of a smile
      tied to so many close calls dodged, outwitted, lucky --
        a beautiful soul --
      if not Hector or Achilles, perhaps Odysseus,
        beloved of gray-eyed Athena
          and of Judy, his patient Penelope.

Poet, story-teller, paddler in water and snow, wanderer, dreamer, father, lover --
    paramour of flashing, tumbling currents
      and roistering streams, huge folding waves, eddying swirls
      to the very last breath --
      the air resonates, pulsating musical waters --
      a stroke of wild heron wings --
        fireworks now, and sweet cut branches
      from the East Fork near Yellow Pine
        and glasses of Dickel raised all around --
          some good words, some tears --

        goodbye, Bill.

ONE LAST VOYAGE ROUND THE HORN

For Ken Brewer, who loved the O'Brien books

The brave stout ships of the line in Nelson's day,
When they had their belly full of iron and shot
And their knees broken so oakum caulking couldn't
Keep water out when winds blew sideways in heavy seas,
And the pumps were manned on every watch and
They couldn't run with the wind as years before,
But griped and wallowed loose in stays like tarts --
They still had hearts of oak and firepower to fight
Belly to belly and foretops locked with that old enemy,
Giving broadside for broadside and ball for deadly ball,
Until, with flags still flying mid heavy smoke and fire
They swirled down together and sank below it all.

That's why we love to read of their brave men.
That's why we smile, to see ourselves in them.

A POEM FOR RAIMOND

for Ray Obermayr, 4-22-2014

He's with his mother now,
whose arms he yearned to know,
as safe in Maggie's arms he lay
a short while ago.

From one love to another
the pilgrim soul may go,
as from the hearts of all of us
into radiant morning sky netted with fire
above dark mountains
his clear voice like a birdsong also goes.

And Ray, Raimond O. -- the man we know --
son, painter, soldier, lover, husband, father, poet, friend --
what happens now
when pulse and breathing end,
we cannot know,
who sit here in the clean light alone
with thoughts collected
in our empty hands --
who loved you so.

THE LUCKY MAN WALKS DOWN THE PERFECT STREET IN PURE SUNLIGHT

Noon. The sun is glinting off the tiny bits of broken glass lying

Here and there on the sidewalk and in the gutters of this most perfect

Street of parked cars and imperfect people on bicycles on foot in a hurry

Passing each other eyes focused into the distance.

$$\text{He looks up into the}$$

Steel blue sky at telephone wires, power lines and airplanes and swooping birds

In a cacophony of car horns, shouts, whistles, laughter, screams, an urgent

Siren's wailing over rooftops and smiles at all of it saying to himself:

Cancer . . . I don't have cancer . . . I don't have cancer.

My wife loves me. My children are safe and happy.

I have just lost my job, but I still have some money

And the sun is shining and anything is still possible.

My teeth don't hurt. My eyesight is clear. My hearing is good.

I can walk without pain, eat most anything I want and piss like a 20 year old.

Oh life, life . . . it is so good to be walking here in sunlight down this perfect street

Surrounded by the urgent surging of everyone else in the world.

What more could anyone wish for?   What more?

190 POUNDS AND DROPPING

Turn away from the cries of the belly
wanting its comfort food
and always a second helping
or a third.

Turn to the hard light,
the simple small bowl half-filled
and once emptied,
forgotten like the night.

There is much to learn
and little time.
The body drags along
like a lame foot,
a whimpering child.

Learn the joy of eating sunlight,
swallowing open air.
The mind and spirit float
high overhead
lightly tethered to forgotten flesh.

Apprentice yourself to poverty,
the path of dirt.
The mind and heart
are luminous
left to themselves,

And all the world
radiant, open
and available to those
who are light
hearted and free.

Like me.

THE LIVING GROVE

Long morning walk, picking up beer cans and windblown trash as I go.

The unspoiled grove, quaken aspen, chokecherry in new leaf
and a fringe of red willow along the edge of the ravine.

I pick my way down the slope and enter it, seeking
to retrieve a beer can I can barely see at the bottom.

Meadow-grass poking new red spear-tips through
the gray straw mat of last year's snow-beaten grasses.

Water splashing, pummeling stones, spring run-off in force,
birds clamoring from branches overhead -- robin, meadowlark.

One beer can, bleached by sun and water, leads to another
and yet another down the steep wash as I penetrate the core.

Stand still on rounded rocks in the sluice of water,
surrounding a stillness ancient and profound.

Where am I? How old? A presence separate and
beyond volition breathes in this elemental place.

Wet stones, bearded grass, willow stalks, horsetail
surround me here. Sunlight flutters the leaves.

At the heart of silence, I shudder and listen.
There is no time. Only light-filled space.

Shake myself free of it. Stoop to retrieve the last beer can
wedged between two stones in the heart of the stream.

Pick my way back up and out to the open road.

AFTERMATH

When the soul is bruised, the world is tender.

Each action has its ache, each touch its pain.

Common things lying around the house --
    books, dishes, the newspaper, old shoes --
        whisper to us --

            you will never be the same!

We walk on tiptoe, on eggshells, on broken feet.

We sit in the corner covering our face with our hands.

The hours go by unnoticed,
            sunlight crossing the wall.

Fatigue finally saps us, and we sleep.

And you pass by all smiles in your joyous world.

    O lucky soul! --
        you idiot! --
            you can't know

what we now know and cannot forget.

How breathing comes to us through broken bones.

THE GREAT TEMPLES

We are sitting in the Salt Lake City airport, my wife and I,
waiting for a flight to Toledo via Dallas and Chicago.
It is mid-day, the weather outside clear and blue.
Our flight will depart "on time." We have no worries.
Jane has her Kindle, I have a heavy book.
All around us people are coming and going quietly.
Departing flights are being announced.
The CNN monitor re-hashes the latest crisis.
It would be easy to doze off for a bit.
But we are praying.

Not out loud, but quietly, in our thoughts.
I am praying for a safe flight and safe return.
And then I am praying for those we are going to visit.
And then I remember our children and grandchildren,
touching each of their names like rosary beads.
I catch a bit of the news as it drones overhead
and pray for Ebola victims, Syrian refugees, flood survivors.
Then I notice the worried expression of a complete
stranger walking briskly toward a gate and into my prayers.
Jane is praying also -- for whom I cannot know.
Her prayers rise and fall with each breath.

It is what we do in airports. All of us.
As we wait for our flights, in suspension for hours it seems,
as we busy ourselves with reading or knitting or newspapers or the
ubiquitous cell-phones, blackberries, iPads, iPhones, laptops
that seem to absorb all consciousness, we are, in fact, still praying.
Behind all surface absorption, our prayers are formed and sent
like brief tweets of hope and worry, blessing and fear.
Although we sit in the most secular buildings on earth -- airports --
in the company of thousands whose lives we cannot know --
we are conformed to an attitude of prayer by patience,
waiting in the vacuum of this neutral space
where thoughts come crowding in and
things we never have time for, things we ignore,
rise up like flowers in the silence.

It is good to be in these places from time to time.
Many who have no church or a temple to pray in,
Some who may never have prayed in their life,
lift up names, worries, concerns and faces,
situations they are escaping from or traveling to meet,
problems that weigh more than their luggage,
released from their shoulders, set on the seat beside them

or the floor at their feet as they lean back and close their eyes.
We send our anxieties into the serene, safe atmosphere
of these airports, where we are anonymous,
and the great structure receives the prayers we proffer
into its benevolent, and non-judgmental space,
giving us back the peace of bland indifference,
a place to rest and recover from the stress of our lives.

Our flight is called, and Jane and I queue up,
take our places in line, hoping the overhead bins aren't full.
We look at our watches, boarding cards firmly in hand.
Around us, on the rows of padded seats,
those who are still waiting do not even notice,
they are so deep in their prayers.

FATIGUE

After a hard day of work,
Exhausted by strife
And tense conversation
And the pressure always to do
More, harder, faster, smarter, yesterday,

I stand in the cool side yard
In early evening.
The valley lights twinkle far below
And moisture filters the light
As the sun goes down.

The branches are stripped
Of their golden fragments
By vagabond winds
Tall grass nods gently
In the meadow across the road.

It seems so natural,
This quiet world,
I can almost believe it is real.

THE WORLDS WE CARRY WITHIN

I was sitting on the basement steps, tying my boots.
The basement wall downstairs was textured and smudged.
I had seen that wall before -- that wall was within me --
far back, before I came to America at two years old --
a wall like that in a stairway leading down
to what? -- I have no idea -- it doesn't matter now.
What matters is an image from sixty years ago,
sparked a thread of chemical memory to light up
in my brain, stirring the mud, and with it
all the lost moments I carry between my ears --
houses and faces, walls and staircases, back alleys, trees, debris
of billions of seconds of sensation stretching slender nerve-chords through
gray folds, none of them scrapped or replaced, each one specific for
color, smell, taste, scent of Dad's aftershave, green soap in the bath-tub dish,
toothpaste, under-arm sweat, mildewed shirts, dry newspaper in drawers,
skylines and steeples, birds perched on branches, footprints in snow
and the boots of two bullies who bloodied my nose at school,
stomping away kicking stones, oh, imagine each person you meet
is carrying so many worlds in their heads they have to walk
carefully, keeping their balance, hands held out like
tightrope walkers teetering over an abyss
and none of the worlds are the same, none are explainable
as if we might unpack our personal universe for others to see --
no, all are locked tight in that unique bone-jar bobbing on our necks
as we tiptoe around, speaking in tongues, untranslatable,
hopeless of ever communicating what we are feeling
or why for no reason at all, looking out a window at a leaf on a branch
we break into tears or run out into the backyard shouting
or turn to the wall for hours, holding our breath
so that nothing escapes, nothing
we would have to explain
to anyone
if it were known.

RAKING THE PEBBLES

This image of an old man raking stones --

    Zen monk at one of the great shrines,

    drawing his wooden tool through rounded pebbles,

    outlining massive rocks and bent fir trees,

    as if confining energies

    of grief and power

    in a field of parallel lines --

reminds me

of my own efforts to

foster peace among competing forces

that ravel my sanity

except for the strict patterns

binding them

in the artifice of ordered

solitude where

what is alive in me

can, for the next moment

or two perhaps

survive.

THE MULTIVERSE

Thursday morning at 7:48 in New York City -- the subway doors close on sixteen separate universes sharing the same space-time continuum unaware of each other

Molly is half asleep after working a double shift at an all night strip club because two girls or quit without notice or were banging the creeps across the street and all she wants is to feed the cat, take a hot bath, sleep till three and not look at another big bellied business man

J.D. is pissed because he left his cell phone on the back of the toilet at the bar and some slimeball has his numbers, and god knows what the sucker will do before he can cancel everything which will take hours he doesn't have since he should already be at work instead of doing

Lucy is tweeting Becky who forwarded a tweet from John (the bastard) about Sarah sleeping with half the football team (really? seriously?) as if they would give her a second look but a scorching tweet comes from Cynthia (the bitch from hell) somebody has to put a cork in her

Fang Li is not reading the newspaper before his face because he is crying because his sister has ovarian cancer and he cannot go home to help but must skin and hang up chickens all day for Mr. Yang who holds his passport and tells him his family is trash she is still so young

Cedric hates that name because it sounds so gay and so British he hates the British their stupid accents corrupt royals and bloody old castles but his mother loved the sound of it but she lives a thousand miles away and only his boss uses it as a joke while his friends just call him Sid

Karin looks at her shoes and tries not to think of the person beside her who smells like a garlic factory and has farted twice as if it were polite she wouldn't be surprised if he stepped on her shoes before they get to the next stop where she'll get off because who would put up with this

Max phones Carlo the "sales puke" who is meeting him for coffee to go over the latest offer from Cramer Cement for the fifteen condo's that are two weeks behind schedule no fault of ours and they better make it right or we'll sue them from hell to breakfast you hear me man?

Alison looks at her reflection in the window as the dark walls flash by and wonders what will happen after death will it be quiet like sleep or will the same world be here with all these crazy people or will it all just dissolve like a pill in a glass of water when she stops breathing

Helen moves the smooth beads through her fingers, lips moving to mouth the prayer over and over silently, her eyes closed, thoughts focused inward as if on her knees she prays for the world with its poor and hungry children, the aged in nursing homes, all victims of violence

Betty lays her head back without caring and closes her eyes. She is too old to be cleaning up offices, dusting desks, mopping floors from midnight to seven, but what can you do when your pension is reduced by those corporate crooks and you have no insurance and rents going up

Nguyen can see how to put oil in the wok and stir in carrots, snow peas, onion, leeks and red pepper, stir for one minute before adding the chopped up chicken, basil leaves, coriander, cumin and some fresh parsley then plating it steaming hot with bean sprouts and fresh basil

Sami her hands in her lap and her mind empty of thinking and the
    slight pressure of her belly against her hands her mind empty
    thinking where she is going and how soon it will be over she knows
    that one way or another she will live with this for the rest of her life
Bud flexes his hands and tightens his biceps, relaxes, tightens and pushes
    up on his toes and relaxes, pushes till his quads burn then relaxes,
    rolls his head around to get the tightness out and flexes his hands so
    the fingers loosen as he plans his routine on the free weights and bench
Fahid wants a cigarette so bad he can taste it can smell the residual smoke
    on the sweater of fellow beside him yellow fingers must be two pack a
    day man but I am stronger than tobacco than alcohol than porn on
    the telly because I can conquer all things in the name of Allah the
Indira does the crossword in the paper she found on the seat because it
    keeps her mind off that afternoon behind the factory when they
    ganged up on her and no one believed she didn't have it coming and
    they got away with it what is an eleven letter word for sonofabitch?
Chad is sweating under his shirt but hopes nobody is noticing how he folds
    his hands across his chest and seems to sleep with his head nodding
    except he is not asleep he is very much awake very much alive very
    much sweating under his shirt where the vest of explosives is waiting for

*Sixteen separate universes in one subway car suddenly interpenetrate each other as
the laws of Newtonian Physics and Quantum Mechanics apply equally everywhere*

THE EMOTOSPHERE

We each move through physical space surrounded
by an invisible projection of attitude and feeling
extended one or two feet on all sides like
the Van Allen Radiation Belts and
Magnetic Field that protect our planet
from cosmic rays, buffer the solar winds
and permit life to survive amid constant threats
from outside. We have to be careful
not to get too close without permission
so our emoto-spheres do not collide
or press with unwanted intimacy
interpenetrating that barrier
between two completely different
world-views and ways of understanding what life is.

POEM FOR SOMEONE WALKING HERE

I am walking under the trees of October in their first turning,

In the leaves falling here and there about me onto the grass,

Touching old stones carved with names I can scarcely read

They are so weather-beaten, softened by decades of rain.

Another lunch hour stroll with moisture rising up from pavement

After the storm cloud passed and the sunlight streams through wet branches

And the leaves tumble wet and gold on the unmowed grass;

Sauntering more than strolling, wandering all directions,

Breathing aromas of wet earth, broken leaves, crushed branches,

And thinking of you, whoever you are, decades from now,

Walking as I do, perhaps on your lunch hour as well,

Taking your soul off the leash, sorting your private sorrows

And letting them fall from your fingers to lie on the grass like leaves.

You will pass ,without giving much thought, a small limestone block

With my name chiseled on it and the dates of my time in the world.

Perhaps you read it with curiosity or amusement, wondering

Who would have such a name and what could this life have been like?

Or perhaps not. No matter. It is enough that I am thinking of you

And that in this thought we are already connected through time,

Who know so little – nothing, really – of each other, and yet

Because we are human and moved by wet leaves falling in sunlight,

Share one heart, one hope, one sorrow, one joy, one dream.

THE CURTIS

PHOTOGRAPHS

SELECTIONS from the photographs of E.S. Curtis, 1868 - 1952

Edward Sheriff Curtis spent thirty years of his life photographing Native American (Indian) tribes west of the Mississippi River.

He began his work in 1896 in Seattle, Washington. His ambition was to capture "the strangeness of Indian life" while the lifestyles of the native peoples were still close to that of their ancestors.

Before finishing his life-work, he had visited eighty tribes and taken over forty-thousand glass plate photographs. Of these, seven hundred and twenty-two were selected for publication in twenty volumes titled The North American Indian.

The following poems are responses to a few photographs from that collection.

THE MUSSLE GATHERER -- SALISH

she works alone
    after the tide is out

fills two hand-woven baskets,
    scraping mussels from the rocks.

she has done this
    in the same way
    for longer than there is memory

her mother
    her grandmother
    the mother of her grandmother

work with her.

THE RUSH GATHERER -- KUTENAI

stillness

the canoe held still
by the rushes

the man intent
on his work

the lake is still
moisture hides the mountains

the fish, the birds
are sleeping

tiny ripples spread out
from the rushes

he is alone
in the surrounding

stillness

THE BLANKET WEAVER -- NAVAHO

the loom stands strong
on the root of the cottonwood tree

she sits at its base
threading the countless strings

mid-morning sun on the cliff-wall
backlights the unthreaded air

it is still quiet and cool
The children and men are away

here she can sing her own songs
here she can hear her own thoughts

the weaving takes care of itself

CANYON de CHELLY -- NAVAHO

our gods are older than stone walls
our gods are taller than canyons

ten thousand rains have washed them
ten thousand floods have worn them

their faces are riven and wrinkled
like faces of ancient warriors

our gods stand silent forever
facing the sun and the dust-storms

they wear the stars for a head-dress
the full moon for a medallion

our gods look out for us always

the People pass safely beside them

FOR A WINTER CAMPAIGN -- APSAROKE

the enemy is sleeping

cold winter morning
snow blowing down the canyon

two braves on horseback
fresh snow coating their blankets

ice blows across their faces
the snow is heavy -- good weather

the enemy is sleeping

horse hooves are silent in snow

now is the time to attack

PRINCESS ANGELINE

-- daughter of Chief Seattle

she has seen too much
    remembers too much

too much has been given
    too much taken away

her kerchief tied under her throat,
    gray hair covers her forehead
    the lines of her mouth turned down
      on a wrinkled chin

no thoughts worth thinking
    no words worth speaking

the eyes say it all:
    too much has been taken away

WAITING IN THE FOREST -- CHEYENNE

a ghostly messenger
      or sheeted corpse

young brave wrapped in white
      stands on the dark path

silent as a beating heart
      that only one can hear

she will come this way

surely she will come

ZUNI GIRLS AT THE RIVER

water jars
balance on their heads
as if attached

two young women
wrapped in black cloaks
at water's edge

so strange
as if from another world
they stand stock still

staring at us

A HOPI GIRL

from the side
        she gazes inward
what we see
        is her hair
combed in perfect discs
        over each ear

like Ozma of Oz
        or Princess Leia
Pre-Raphaelite angel
        elegant in silence

simple white beads
        for a choker

who is she thinking of?

ANDRES CANYON

in a guarded ravine
        screened by a massive palm

she kneels at the stream
        touching one hand to the water

face averted
        full breast pendant
        above the bare knees

a private place
        for bathing
        or contemplation

or waiting
        for him to find her

AS IT WAS IN THE OLD DAYS

summer on the plains

bison shedding their pelts
        rest peacefully in grass

calves close to the cows
        the old bulls dozing off

they have no enemies
        the breeze carries no warning

a sunny afternoon
        that lasts a million years

what is that
        moving on the horizon?

THE OFFERING -- SAN ILDEFONSO

on point
at the cliff face

one brave
sprinkles seed to the wind

chanting his medicine song
addressing the gods

we don't know what he is asking
be it rain or good hunting

there is only this human being
beseeching infinity

against all odds

CHIEF JOSEPH -- NEZ PERCE

the strong face masks its sorrows
      metal disc ear-rings
      loops of white beaded necklace

all the long marches in winter
      pushing the People
      over the high passes

      not far enough
      not far enough

stoic now, accepting
      what cannot be changed
      eyes holding onto their sorrows

the dignified, human face
      one day, one hour
      one more twist of the trail

      how far would be far enough?

ATSINA WARRIORS

eight war chiefs
      gathered on horseback
      in beads, deerskins, war-bonnets

well met on the desolate plains

a light breeze
      blows hair and feathers sideways
      some face the camera
      others away

keeping their souls to themselves

just a class photo for history's year-book
      no battles today

the breeze
      stirs the tails of their ponies

BEAR'S TEETH -- ARIKARA

look at me
as I now look at you

face to face
eye to eye
warrior to warrior

I am not afraid

I am not a slave

there is still light in my eyes

look at me
look into my eyes

I am a free man

ON THE LITTLE BIGHORN -- APSAROKE

a hot afternoon
        big bend in the river

clutch of white tipi's
        meat drying on racks
        clothes drying in the sun

siesta time
        lying in the cool shadows

the ponies
        are up to their bellies in water

life is good

life is good

KUTENAI DUCK HUNTER

the twin-tipped canoe

rests like a leaf on the water

making no ripples

mists of morning

cover the distant mountains

nothing is moving

even the rushes are still

wait and listen

listen   wait

hear them?

they are almost here

THE BIRDS OF GOD

THE BIRDS OF GOD

The birds of God fly overhead.
They swoop and flurry in flocks,
Dipping sudden to a stand of trees,
Then flittering off again across the fields.

The birds of God come to the feeder
For their daily seed -- opportunists!
They feed on what they do not grow
But trust, somehow, will be provided.

They revel in snow, these birds of God,
And sing from icy fence-posts as if
On salary in some self-appointed choir
Proclaiming joy and freedom all day long.

And when I am most discouraged,
Down in heart about this life and what
One single soul can do to heal the world --
They surround me like a living testament.

I am lifted up in laughter by their song,
Carried forward by their furious wings.
These birds of God are my evangelists --
Facing the storm on the tip of an evergreen!

Oh birds of God, you never fail to sing!
And Grace descends like snowfall on your wings.

AT THE FEEDER

The small ones come first --
sparrows, house finches, siskins --
just after first light.

They send a scout ahead
to flit from their roost in the chokecherries,
stitching the cold air
with a flutter and glide, flutter and glide
to the top of the swing-set,
then to the spruce
and then to the feeder if the coast is clear.

One whistle brings the others in a flock.
They are a gossipy bunch,
swooping down from all sides to chatter
at the screened sunflowers,
turret of thistle seeds
and the long plastic tube of mixed grains.

Battering and flattering about,
zipping off to perch,
sweeping back to push a fellow aside,
all in good humor,
glad for the morning and sunshine
on dandelions or snow-banks,
keeping a look-out
for the neighbor's feral cat.

Then, just as they arrived --
WHOOSH! -- they scatter in all directions
as the black-birds come cawing in,
or magpies, flying skunks,
mawkishly break up the party like Hell's Angels.

Then it is quiet, until noon or four o'clock,
with only a few chickadees
lazily dropping by to sort the strewn seeds
and take a private splash
in the bird-bath.

NOTES FOR A LIFE-LIST

The downy woodpecker
gives up pecking the power pole,
selects one sunflower seed
to carry to the round rail of the fence.

He breaks it with his beak.
Then comes for another.

*

The tree swallows,
husband and wife,
check out all three
blue-bird boxes
before selecting the one
furthest from the feeders
to build their nest.

They are a tight team,
one cruising the field
for mosquitoes and flies,
cutting quick corners
and cookies in air,
while the other stands
guard against magpies.

Once they fledge two offspring,
they're off to Disneyland.

*

The kingbird couple
build their nest of twigs and straw
in the storm-gutter at the end of the roof.

They cackle and squawk like New Yorkers
whenever I walk in the yard,
one hovering overhead
until I turn on the sprinkler and leave.

Fearless as pit-bulls,
I have seen them chase a hawk
across the alfalfa field,
badgering and pecking from both sides.

They kick their young from the nest
to flutter and fall and hopefully learn to fly.

*

Hummingbirds hover
with a buzz like a light-saber
warning all challengers.

When courting
they soar straight up to the roof
then dive straight down to the pavement
aqain and aqain.

It gets one's attention.
While they are performing
the Bullock's orioles suck the feeders dry.

*

Eagles and hawks,
goldens and red-tails,
ride on the thermals
hour after hour,
diving down sudden
to pounce on a gopher
or pluck a young sparrow
from the top of the spruce tree.

And one summer morning
I watched helplessly
as the neighbor's black cat,
having found no birds at the feeder,
took a run up the hayfield
where a golden eagle stood preening.

I thought, "Oh kitty, kitty . . . "
But the eagle just lifted off and flew away.

*

Two sand-hill cranes
graceful as kites
drop to the hayfield to dance --
leaping and flapping
and lifting long legs,
and squawking their passionate love song.

*

One winter morning
I strapped on the snowshoes
and stamped out a path up the hay-field
to pitch a bucket of chick-scratch
in a golden arc over the drifts
near the chokecherries
where a family of pheasants
sheltered like refugees
trapped by the wind-driven snow.

I stood catching my breath
and surveying my "Kingdom,"
(meaning the entire valley spread out below
from Malad to Pocatello)
when a gray owl roosting in a half-dead tree
suddenly spread wings and
cruised like a stealth bomber over my head
without making a sound.

When I recovered my breath,
I remembered
whose kingdom it was.

COURAGE

They teach me courage,
these small birds.

They have no past, no future,
only this spark
of fully attentive being.

Seek - seek - seek - and find.
Be wary, but not
fearful, follow your heart.

Find mates, find seeds, fly high --
enjoy your wings.
Death is always unexpected

like flying full speed into a glass window.

SUMMER SOLSTICE

The sky begins to brighten at four a.m.
By five, the birds are waking up and cackling.
Light sifts into the fields beneath the mountain
Like silver dust coating the alfalfa.
The stars are gone, the sky a silken sheen,
As softly, quietly, earth receives the morning.

Another day -- just that -- a measure of life,
Profound as all eternity, common as breath,
And I, one witness, sit in my small place,
Part of the flawless spinning of time and space.

THE ASPEN GROVE

Walking home
I pass the aspen grove,
melted clean of snow.
Fresh spears of urgent green
Piercing the flat gray stems of winter grass.

In the soft meadow,
Light of the setting sun
Warms the opening trees.
Brewer's black-birds settle in the top branches,
Cackling, bickering, rowdy with songs of spring.

I think of Breughel
And the Elder Cranach.
Something in the light,
And the curve of the harrowed field,
Something permanent
Of the earth.

How old it feels to be alive.

ACCEPTANCE

Fresh snow overnight, and now the moon
        Half gone, wanes in the west
        Over mountain ridges newly pinked
                With first sunlight,
           Rose tipped above crushed azure.
              The dark fir tree
              In foreground,
On all sides, fresh snow filling my footsteps,
        Old sins erased,
              The world made new,
                    An illusion of creation.

    There is no one else to share this with.

Having accepted that,
        I am at peace with all things,
        With death and the going into dust,
              Into nothing, unknown,
           Taking with me only
              The half-empty moon,
        And the memory
           Of your eyes
              That I have loved,

    The soft morning snow filling my footsteps.

THIS DAY

There is only this day,
whatever it brings.

Even a life of ninety years
is given day by day by day.

This day -- now -- the
moment of being alive.

We are foolish to want more.
There is no more. This day

is what we have. Take it.

FIRST HINTS

A sense, a whisper, the first hint --
early light on the snowfields,
the road half clear and tire tracks
frozen in dirt that softens by midday.

Though still in winter's fist,
the heart takes hope,
a smile, a song, a quickened step --
the end of it in sight --
over the next hill, past
the next patch of icy mornings.

Birdsong, a freshening breeze --
green shoots, breaking the icy crust,
buds projecting their extravagant phalloi
on limb-tips of the aspen trees.

SOLILOQUY ON THE AUGUST MOON

Night of the august moon
Yellow as a peach from the fires.
Night of crickets and early stars,
the moonlight brightening as it ascends
And silver air cool through the windows,
The whisper of the distant traffic and the trains . . .

Oh I will forget the body and these sixty-five years.
In my heart I am always adolescent..
The man outside bows to the boy within.
Together they can still dream anything.

In their world, luminous poems are rising,
Breaking the surface of the universe tonight
To breach like blue whales in the strong moonlight.

We sit on the patio watching, my self and I.

SOLILOQUOY OF THE SURVIVING SPOUSE

When you no more are living at my side
And I must face each morning on my own,
I am consoled by all the things we loved,
And in their presence I am not alone.

The bird that pecks a seed outside the sill,
The flowers that glory in the morning sun,
Majestic clouds that sweep across the hills,
The light-filled trees, the countless stars, the moon.

In all these things we loved I find your face,
That through our loving what we are remains
To be discovered by the eye that sees,
Touched and suffered by the heart that feels.

Through tears and silence all these things sustain
My love of you, our love of all that's real.

MY LOVE

Always the strong one
        you chose and did not change,
        you knew how to love
            and not discard life's gift.

I was weak and waffling,
        blown this way and that
           by every wind
      except you anchored me.

You taught me how love waits,
        enduring much,
            trusting in the end.
      I owe my life to you,

      My wife. My friend.

THE CONSOLATION OF POETRY

We cannot change the world or change mankind,
Nor even change ourselves to much degree.
So much that happens is beyond our power
To influence or improve, had we the mind,
Or inclination to avoid, could we but see
Its coming and knew the day and hour.

Instead we suffer, along with all the rest,
The wounds inflicted randomly by chance
Within the mad machinery of our lives;
And yet consoled by poetry, by singing blessed,
By words drawn inward in ecstatic dance,
We find the strength and humor to survive.

We arm ourselves with poems, dreams and songs
To face life's 'slings and arrows' and be strong.

TO BE A FRIEND

For Harry Shimada Jr.

To be a friend transcends theology.
To be a friend precedes all history.
It is the thread connecting all that live,
this reaching out, this smile, this generosity.

To be a friend is inexplicable --
beyond self-interest, family, duty, principle,
risking it all in one spontaneous response.
To be a friend is primal, utterly simple.

To be a friend is what you are for me,
despite all things on which we disagree --
religion, politics, manners -- chaff in the wind.
When no one else was, you were there for me.

I haven't forgotten and will not to the end,
your face, your smile, your eyes. You are my friend.

THE TREASURIES OF THE SNOW

Job 38: 22

Drifts pile heavy on the windward banks,
deposited by a three-day blizzard and blow.

Desert people, desperate for summer water, know
how precious these huge drifts that melt for months.

This afternoon I skied beneath a cornice
massive as a frozen wave, remembering
the scouring winds that shaped it weeks ago.

In bright sunlight, with irreligious joy,
I skimmed across the treasuries of the snow.

SNOWFALL ON MOUNTAINS

Wraiths of shredded mist drift past the mountains.

Snowfall, early morning, like manna flakes.

The fields are deep with it, and the dry stalks of flowers.

The ski area halfway hides its rocky slopes and steep draws.

On top, the firs are powdered like confection.

Christmas is coming. Listen, listen.

It is so still you can hear snowflakes colliding.

A FEW DAYS BEFORE CHRISTMAS

Clear December morning, windless, still.

Grove of aspens, every limb and leaf, still.

Crusted snow-banks, resigned and still.

Mountains above and across the valley, still.

Shafts of yellow straw in wells of snow, still.

Two sparrows hide in the sagebrush and are still.

Leaning on my stick, holding my breath, stock-still.

Still here. Still together. Still alive.   Still.

LIGHT SNOW, NO WIND

The fir tree and the house across the road
are veiled by the thin slanting snow.
The morning birds cluster and hop by the feeder
and one vagrant pheasant, scarcely visible,
pecks at chick-scratch on the hayfield drifts.

Quiet in the house, coffee in the kitchen,
gray light, snow light, dusts the potted plants.
The Christmas pyramid in the living room stands still.
Somewhere in background, soft tinkling carols
accompany the moment, silent, reflective.

The passing years hang on a pointed star
twirling slowly from a thin string in the garage.
Nothing left to sing or send, to bake or wrap or do.
Sit in the solitude of snowfall, fresh and new.

SOLSTICE SLEEP

The darkest night of the year
has passed in peaceful sleep.
The small gift sacks my wife prepared
have all been passed out to the neighbors
and our friends from out of town stopped by
to give us season's greetings last evening
before we turned off all the lights and slept.
The wind was calm and no new snow came down.
The darkness folded round the house like sleep
and dreams, whatever they were, rose quietly,
drifted down through starlight and settled into the dark
so nothing disturbed the long hours of the night.
I lie awake at seven, in the snow-dim dawn,
happy to have voyaged safely into the realm of light.

HOLY WEEK

The winter's snow-banks are receding, Lord.
The snow-bridges crumble into the ravines.
The drifted aspens stand in widening wells
as snow retreats each day from meadow and field.
The first birds perch on wet fence-posts and sing,
where caps of ice were melting days ago.
The sun-washed fields reveal the blackened furrows
where winter wheat thrusts up brave blades of green.
The kingdoms of frost and stinging wind relent,
releasing softness, rain, blossoms, forgiveness and mud.
A freshening breeze proclaims life's resurrection.
I walk the softened road like a man reborn.

Ave! Ave! Christi, crucified king!
My soul stands on its fence-post perch and sings!

LENT

Sometimes I feel
The weight of all my sins,
Knowing now, on reflection,
As a man of years,
How much real damage I inflicted
On those I love.
Didn't think of it then --
Can't forget it now.
Words carelessly spoken,
Curses, temper, flash in the pan,
Reckless, self-driven, thoughtless choices,
Hurting wife, daughter, son,
Wounds long past,
No way now
To reconcile or repair
Except God heal them in His way
Beyond understanding.

Confessed, forgiven, yes --
But still one bears
The weight of what was said and done
And cannot be changed.

Live a long life and
You'll carry a heavy load,
Until it brings you to your knees
In the middle of the road.

HOLINESS

The sun rises in the northeast notch,
Blinding me as I read in the easy chair,
Blinding my eyes to the blurred words on the page,
Commanding inner attention, worship, prayer,
Acknowledgement of Presence and of power,
Holiness, movement, brightness, Being --
Pure light giving life to all that breathe --
The Lord -- Adonai -- El Elyon -- El Shaddai -- Yahweh --
The Nameless One too deep for comprehension.
Now meadowlarks rise singing from the hayfield.
The sky is clear and clean and full of hope.
I have no words to offer, nothing to add,
But open my hands to receive whatever is given,
Open my eyes, my heart, my mind, to receive it all.

THE GREAT ECCLESIA

Sometimes during our closing prayers
At Thursday morning men's Bible study,
As each man offers in turn a few quiet words
Of blessing or thanksgiving, supplication for a friend
Or family member or the suffering world,
I feel the presence of the Great Ecclesia --
Body of all believers, living and dead --
Who trust in the One who died and rose again
And through all ages call upon His name
To heal and bless, to enter broken lives
And bring -- by inexplicable miracle -- peace
And new hope and the fresh start of forgiveness,
So wherever two or three or a thousand are assembled,
The ineffable, invisible Ecclesia of believers surrounds us all.

LITANY FOR A DARK DAY

Remind me, Lord, how blessed I am.
When uncertainty, doubt and worries overwhelm
remind me of your saving grace, your power.

When days feel empty and meaningless,
when I am alone, friendless, in despair for hours,
remind me Lord, how blessed I am.

When past sins and failures overwhelm
and I recall lost chances to be kind,
remind me of your saving grace, your power

When I have no reason to get out of bed,
no work, no urgent task, no ambition and no hope,
remind me, Lord, how blessed I am.

The true terrors have not happened.
The devastating catastrophe has not come.
Remind me of your saving grace, your power.

What sufferings I have are small indeed
compared to others, compared to many I know.
Remind me, Lord, how blessed I am.

In all things you are faithful and kind.
You have not abandoned me even for an hour.
Remind me, Lord, how blessed I am.
Remind me of your saving grace, your power.

ONE IN THE SPIRIT

Somewhere in North Korea tonight
a poet is writing in a secret notebook
that is hidden by day behind a brick in the wall.
I reach out to him or her as if we knew each other.

The violin sonatas of J.S. Bach
are played publicly or privately
in every country on earth, the musicians
sharing together that one great heart and mind.

This week in China, a warehouse exploded.
Some of the firemen running toward it
were killed in the second blast. Firefighters
the world over ache for their grieving families.

It is the same with every craft and skill.
Artisans have empathy for each other.
They know the risks and joys no others can know
and when one suffers, everybody weeps.

So it is for all who breathe the air,
who hunger to stride freely down the street,
to paint and dance and sing at the top of our voices.
When one of us can't breathe, we breath for them.

Beyond barriers of language, religion, politics --
one spirit inspires the passions that we share.
A young man carrying two sacks confronts a tank.
We stand beside him in Tiananmen Square.

MEETING JESUS AT THE MAVERICK STATION

A blustery night, late September. I stopped
at the Maverick station near the Interstate,
after playing bluegrass for a few hours with friends,
to use the restroom, buy a sack of chips
and a creamy coffee for the long ride home.

I saw him sitting by the entry door,
yellow wind-breaker, hood up, blue jeans, boots,
his arms around his knees, scruffy pack off to one side.
Judged him to be mid-twenties, a bit too lean and
probably needing a hand-out or a ride.

He was just another mother's son, perhaps
a prodigal, busted flat and heading back to Dad,
running from a dead-end job, bad weather or a woman,
or maybe just one of the redeemed, trusting God
to move him toward what he was waiting for.
His eyes were confident, his grin relaxed,
brown hair to his shoulders and a ten day beard.

I went on in and did what I came to do.
Passed him on the way out with a quick glance.
He smiled and I smiled back. No words, no sign,
no hand held out or thumb stuck in the air.
He seemed contented just be sitting there,
and I went on around him to my car.

It was only when stopped at the left turn light
for the Interstate onramp heading south
that I realized who he was. I turned
at the next interchange and hurried back.
I should have stopped to talk, bought him dinner,
given him a ride wherever he wanted to go.

When I got back to the Maverick, he was gone.
The one he had been waiting for had come
and I drove home wondering what I had missed.

THE GOLDEN TREE

I stand beneath a golden tree
and let its lessons fall on me.

Each sun-soaked flake, perfect, complete
tumbles gently to my feet.

The promise in each yellow leaf
consuming joy, subsuming grief

fills up my head, buries my feet,
my heart as open as a street

where on a sunny afternoon
I stand beneath a golden dome

in aural silence, foot to crown,
the Presence of the Holy One.

THE MOSAIC

Remembering Ray Obermayr

The ones we live with, great and small,
surround us with their influence, as we with ours
connect to each in unintended ways, despite
our will to change for good or ill. The real bonds
are formed by what we are; connections last
long after all our conscious deeds are lost.
This living web connecting face to face,
and heart to eye and hand to outstretched hand
is fixed in time and set within the space
of the expanding moment, binding our bright souls
like chips of colored tile to the vaulted walls,
ceiling and floor in patterns none can see,
except, one step removed, we finally stand
on the porches of Eternity -- and see them all.

SONG OF UNDESERVED BLESSING

I wake five minutes before the alarm, late January, dark,
pull on socks, sweatpants, old shirt, slippers, still half asleep,
stand by the large window facing the mountain range
and survey the hayfields whitened with fresh snow.

The furnace turns on quietly. How happy I am.
The water in the pipes is not frozen.
The pump works, despite sub-zero temps.
Electricity circulates in the walled veins of the house.

I take nothing for granted anymore.
My own body, sixty-two years against the odds and I am
healthy, standing upright without pain, joyful, lucid,
even losing a few pounds and feeling good.

I know how blessed this is -- how lucky I am.
The woman I love is blessed also,
sleeping in her sleigh bed under covers and quilt,
warm and happy, she dreams about gardens in spring.

It is not so lucky for others in this world.
My friend who suffers nursing home isolation,
two amputations, storms of delusion, rage and sorrow,
riding the fierce ship of his body into the maelstrom.

Others, so many of them, coping with lives
unfairly broken, damaged bodies, lost careers, families forsaken,
not to speak of the numberless without food or homes,
who are always on my heart and in my mind.

I can't forget the sorrows I can't solve,
but standing here, in darkness, this winter morn,
I also can't forget how blessed I am,
and thank the Nameless One that I was born.

THANKSGIVING

I have spent enough time
           in the house of desolation
to be thankful it is not my daily home.

I have tasted enough crumbs
           from the bitter loaf of sorrow
to be thankful it is not my daily bread.

I have wandered enough miles
           through the wilderness of terror
to be thankful it is not my destination.

I have pondered long enough
           on the ruins of my scheming
to be thankful they are not the promised land.

           for deliverance from fear
           for this common quiet day
           for the mysteries of prayer
           for all I can't explain away
                      and do not understand

I get down on my knees and raise my hands.

WAKING THOUGHTS ON A SUNLIT MORNING

When this breathing being, myself, will cease
to breathe, and being itself dissolve to nothingness --

     the moment, unimaginable, absurd, impossible,
     as I have always been myself, alive,
     and striding gladly through the morning air
     without a thought that I should ever die --

when this unthinkable moment suddenly arrives,
and thought and dream and expectations cease
their hammering heart-beat dancing breath by breath --

     what then? surprise? denial? disbelief? despair?
     the mind collapsing like a circus tent, the eyes
     fixed on a blown-out candle-flame, the vagabond soul
     departing parted lips, and I myself vanished, gone, but where?

a shimmer of sparks spun soft on the morning air . . .

PRAYERS FROM THE FIRE

EVERYDAY INTO THE FIRE

Remembering 9/11/2001

So we go forth, each of us, wherever we are
Into the unknown events prepared for us each day,
Expecting the routine grind of meetings and tasks,
But knowing as well each day could be our last.
So those who left for offices in the twin towers
As they had for so many days and years, grabbing
A cup of coffee or a bagel on their way, thinking
Their normal Tuesday thoughts, phone calls to make,
Agendas and meetings to plan, presentations to give,
And found themselves suddenly in the heart of the fire.
So those also who ran not away, but directly into
Stairwells, climbing with axes and fire gear
To help, to rescue, as they had been trained,
Without time for terror, driven by desperate hope
And felt the world collapse on top of them.

So each of us, with trepidation borne of
New awareness of the risks we face, step forth
Onto airplanes, into tall buildings, cars on freeways,
Subway tunnels, ships at sea, crossing the street
Where strangers with well-calculated plans
Count down their coordinated attacks
That we cannot anticipate, but must face
With courage born of fire from within
The unexpected terror around the corner,
As those who said 'let's roll' plunged the plane,
Or holding hands in black smoke holocaust
Leapt forth like desperate angels into fiery air.

Thus we face our lives, come fire or death.
And honor their lost lives with every breath.

OF AESCHELUS AND SOPHOCLES

The Greeks described it centuries ago --
Hubris, that careless arrogance
Of rich and powerful men who act alone,
Defying history and the ancient gods,
Dragging entire nations into ruin.

        I'm not right in my head anymore.
        They've just beheaded another American in Iraq.
        No matter the thousands we bombed to death,
        This brutal image severs consciousness.
        I feel Damascus steel on my neck.

So we stand upon this desolate plain,
Caught in a place we did not wish to go,
Lead by leaders whom we did not choose.
The gods who drive us now are not our gods.
They kick us as we strain against the leash.

OUR LADY OF GUANTANAMO

Trees still exist, and there are still clouds.
Sunlight falls in plenitude mixed with rain.
Birds are free to come and go overhead,
Beyond high fences and concertina wire.
In the yard, the faceless persons shuffle
In orange jumpsuits, sweltering, alive,
Although there is no world for them to touch
Or be touched by. They have no names.
Sometimes a radio sneaks in from far away,
Rattling its thin music, paper on a comb.
Never any word from the lost world of
Cities, busses, cars, apartments, families.
Their world is elemental -- sun, rain, sky.
They are permitted to breathe the air,
Eat some nameless food and pass it through,
Shuffle aimlessly in shackled legs, the
Body kept alive, but not the soul.

Their souls turn inward and upward, into
The hands of Our Lady of Guantanamo,
Who looks upon each one in every hour,
Who sees them in the interrogation cells,
Naked in the hot dark, cold at night,
Sees them weeping, angry, frightened,
Knows what is done to them each day
And who is doing it. She does not judge,
Extends her gentle hands above their heads
In perpetual brokenhearted prayer, as over
The broken body of her only child, hurt
Beyond years, strong beyond sacrifice,
She prays the names of every human being
On each side of the wire, holding
All their loneliness in her hands.

VISION OF CHRIST AT ABU GHARIB

Stripped before the taunting guards,
Attack dogs snarling at his crotch,
His bloody hands stretched out,
Bearded, long-haired head hanging,
Shoulders slumped beneath the truncheon,
He is any naked, helpless human being,
Any hopeless mother's son humiliated.
The soldiers finish up their dirty games --
The peaked, black hood pulled over his head,
Arms spread wide beneath a black poncho,
Fingers pinned to electric wires, bare feet
On the box above wet pavement --
From the watchtower of the waiting cross
With eyes that see the jackals of the world,
The lips keep speaking the impossible --

"Abba, Father, even these . . . "

LEGACY

The United States is increasing aid to Laos to help remove
unexploded ordinance that continues to kill people thirty years
after the end of the Vietnam War. Over two million tons of bombs
were dropped on Laos from 1964 to 1973 – double the amount
dropped on Germany in WWII. The bombs have killed over
6,000 Laotians since the end of fighting and maimed countless
others. Nearly a third of the bombs failed to explode, lying in
wait as "de facto anti-personnel mines." (AP news story 12/27/04)

Many of the pilots who flew those missions are gone.
Of those who remain -- no one can speak for them.
Soldiers follow orders and do what they must
And live as best they can with the aftermath.
Many of the missions were flown at night.
The targets were triangulations of geography.
There is no way to judge how successful a mission was
Except that you dumped your load and got out safe,
And there were some who didn't come back.
What it was like on the ground is another nightmare.
Best leave it alone and just get through the day.

After thirty years, it is possible finally,
For our government to reclaim some of its property --
The unexploded bombs it never dropped
On the people who were never there
But continue stumbling onto them and dying --
Your tax dollars still at work.

WHEEL OF FORTUNE

It is the fourth anniversary of the war.
I am watching *WHEEL OF FORTUNE* with my wife.
Pat Sajak is standing there, all smiles,
And Vanna, trim and sexy as always,
Transforms letters with her magic touch
As three very excited ladies clap their hands,
Spin the wheel in turn and jump for joy.

It is an ancient wheel that we spin.
Most segments are good to land on it seems.
They give a little money and another chance.
Some have prizes, exotic cruises, sports cars.
Only a few are disappointing -- you lose a turn
Or even go completely bankrupt for awhile.
The thrill comes from barely missing disaster
While with each spin the audience gasps and shrieks.

Then there is the heavy wheel in Iraq.
You get up, go out and give it a careful spin,
Hoping not to stop beside a car that detonates
Or end up in a street market or a mosque
At the exact moment a martyr enters paradise.
Not much chance of money on that wheel.
Just getting home alive is reward enough.
You clap your hands. You weep.
You jump, almost, for joy.

THE HEART IS A BLACK SITE

The mind recoils from all that is not right
With righteous indignation at the news,
But not the heart -- the heart is a black site.

The heart has motives that won't bear the light,
Blood-steeped tribal memories that choose
Dark deeds the mind rejects as not being right.

The mind seeks perfect justice and will fight
For every innocent victim of abuse.
Not so the heart -- the heart is a black site.

It renders enemies in furnaces by night,
Leaving piles of spectacles, teeth and shoes
That gag the gentle mind, obsessed with right,

Crusading nobly in print to protest the plight
Of Rwandans, Chechnians, Bosnians, Palestinians, Jews --
While the heart works fiercely in its pitch-black site,

Dispensing vengeance, repaying slight for slight,
Till every evil doer receives his due.
The mind breaks down, accepting might as right,
And serves the heart, the implacable black site.

But not tonight, by God -- not tonight.

OF DUTY AND HONOR

Even now, at the end of their lives,
Surviving veterans of WWII can seldom share
What they suffered and what they know of war
With children, grandchildren -- those who were not there.
Vietnam vets, too, just shake their shaggy heads,
Gripping hands with buddies at POW MIA gatherings.
And the recent troops, returned from the gulf wars
To heal from wounds and repair disrupted lives,
Avoid the cameras, step politely away instead,
In unspoken union with the living and dead.

So it has always been throughout time.
Those who train to risk their lives in battle,
Whether enlisted soldiers, conscripts or draftees,
Enter the ranks of those who live under orders,
Who go where they must and do commanded tasks,
Without hesitation or giving second thought,
In dirty, dangerous corners of the world.

Their dreams are always of their families.
Commanding officers may deserve respect,
Or not -- Commanders in Chief come and go --
And politicians merit less than scorn
For careless ignorance, petty ambition, greed.
So it has always been throughout time.

One thing remains unchanged for those in ranks --
Their loyalty to their unit and to each other,
Out of duty and a sense of personal honor
That overmasters terror in the face of death.
That they be found worthy of their comrades,
And equal to the task they face together;
Despite egregious, impossible circumstance,
That they push forward, prevail, survive, defeat or die
And in that terrible striving are so annealed
In the shedding and losing of lifeblood
That they can never again be separated,
Nor can another ever enter their circle.

Of duty and honor, nothing is revealed
Except to those who have striven on the field.

THE GRIST MILL

Those in the middle of it, caught
Between the stones, who cannot escape
The opposing forces in their inexorable grinding
Against each other, with bullets and bombs,
These people get ground down
To pulp, to fiber and blood
By the relentless work of that machinery.

And we who watch this process,
Also between the stones
Of a government we do not control,
We also get ground down
By the killing of others committed in our name.

These massive stones, once set in motion,
Never cease their mindless grinding
Till all the energy driving them is spent,
And all the grain exhausted, no more
Armies, cities, country-folk, riches or resources left
To be crushed into the oil of victory.
The stones are dumb – they merely grind away.
They have no malice, only momentum.

O pray for people caught between the stones.
O pray those who set the stones in motion.

THE LAST HELICOPTER

By the time it was over
And he was writing the history,
Thucydides knew more than anyone alive
About wars of self destruction.
But we have not bothered
To read his words.

Before the last helicopter
Lifts off from the last unburned high-rise
In the Green Zone, desperate people
Clinging to its skids and others
Jumping off the rooftop
In despair, we must
Witness a few more scenes
Of ancient tragedy --
A Tet offensive perhaps,
A winter attack in the Ardennes
Catching sleeping armies by surprise,
Or Hannibal crossing the Alps with elephants.

We will, of course, leave everything behind --
Tons of heavy equipment, armor, artillery, tanks,
Humvees, files of unshredded secret documents,
Computer hard drives and more than enough
Abandoned ordinance to equip two armies for civil war.

And the people left behind,
Who trusted us, but could not get away
In the final chaotic scramble after the perimeter fell,
What happens to them is also written down
In the unsentimental records
Of lost wars.

We will come home, lick our wounds,
Write our history books about lessons learned,
And swear to each other -- "never again!"

And in twenty years the next young buck,
Eager to muscle a place for himself in the history books,
Having never heard of Thucydides,
Will try his luck.

THE PEOPLE YOU ARE KILLING COULD BE FRIENDS

Turning away from the news too terrible to bear --
The latest suicide truck bomb in a market-place,
Or accidental air strike on a school outside Kandahar,
Abduction, torture and murder of office workers --
I think always of the faces of the victims --
Men, women, children, old and young --
And know I would have loved them, had we met.
Such beautiful eyes, white teeth, open smiles,
Such colorful clothing, headscarves, earrings, hats and shoes.
Left to ourselves, meeting by chance in a market
Or in a coffee shop or at the home of a mutual friend,
We would have quickly broken through the artificial barriers
Of language and custom, how to bow and shake hands,
And shared something to eat and drink and a story
Of where we came from, what we do, and found
In almost every case, a common thread --
A friend, a city visited, even perhaps a relative --
And in the course of a few hours, become good friends.
This has happened in my travels time and again.
Always the same miracle -- strangers blossoming into friends.
And now, with each day's news, I am unsettled.
Life is short and we don't have too much time.
So many beautiful souls are being destroyed.

The part of me you can't see runs down the street,
Driven mad by war that never ends,
Shouting at the top of my voice --
                                   Stop it! Stop it!
The people you are killing could be friends!

PRAYERS FROM THE FIRE

As you pray, so shall you be.

Though you stand in the fire,

Though you sink in the sea.

The heart's pure desire

Becomes purest prayer,

Thus even in fire, the Almighty is there,

The small, inner voice conquers all fear,

The undeserved grace answers all prayer.

Wherever you are, in fire or in sea,

As you pray, so shall you be.

GARAGE SALE

GARAGE SALE

And so, after all these years, we open up our lives
like a person having a garage sale on a Saturday morning.
We push up the rolling door and reveal the clutter of decades,
floor to ceiling, wall to wall, in the space where a car has never parked.
Put ads in the newspaper, tape signs to the light poles:
GARAGE SALE!! GREAT DEALS!! DAWN TILL DARK!!

And our friends and the neighbors stop by, along with the
early birds -- professionals, antique collectors, serious shoppers --
to have a free cup of coffee, frosted donut, chocolate chip cookie
and browse the tables spread with forty years of treasures --
worn lampshades, retired furniture, incomplete table-settings,
text books not opened since college, ancient exercise equipment,
xcountry ski contraptions, spinning cycles, hand-weights, yoga mats,
residue of good intentions gone astray, squatty analog television sets,
outdated generations of computers, rotary dial phones, VHS recorders,
even an eight-track stereo and a stack of scratchy vinyl discs,
always a manual typewriter, heavy as a boat-anchor,
on which poems, novels, Masters theses were hand-typed
with carbon copies or mimeo stencils, medieval technologies inconceivable
to youngsters who post a quizzical photo on Facebook
as if touring an exhibit of dinosaurs.

We invite you to pass over it all with mildly amused disinterest,
the jumbled leftovers of eighteen thousand days.
Brush over gently with absent-minded fingertips
and discover suddenly an item you have been searching for
without hope of ever finding -- here! -- in a dark corner --
underneath a heap of bric-a-brac -- the ceramic Italian fruit bowl
like the one on your grandmother's side-board -- in almost
perfect condition, the glaze scarcely freckled, the Mediterranean colors
once dust is wiped away still fresh and intense -- oh my! --
but the price? Careful now. Do they know its value?
Marked at $3.00. Will they take $1.50? Yes! Oh, my!

This is as close as you get, those who might think
you are coming to know us by rummaging through relics
worn out by our living. The family secrets are squirreled away
in the folds of the brain and the heart's locked valves
that not even poetry penetrates. There the true
life aches, losses, disappointments, and triumphs
lie in dark corners, like Freudian furniture under wraps,
discovered only on dark nights when new wreckage
of careless pride, venal desire or original sin
tumbles in to be buried beneath consciousness.

Abandon hope, all sleuths armed with psychic guile.
Instead of an insight, you'll get an inscrutable smile.

For the rest of this garbage, we don't care a fig.
Either you buy it today or it goes to the Good Will Store.
Make an offer, wangle a bargain, score big on a three-headed
monkey lamp or a silver-plate dancing elephant with sapphire eyes!
Dig through a leather-bound sea chest to discover a prize!
Find that matching teacup to complete your set,
or what appears to be a genuine shrunken head
with eyes sewn shut and a bamboo spike through the nose,
brought back by Great Uncle Sidney from the tribes of Borneo.
There's plenty of interesting trash on the tables and shelves,
boxes of puzzles, buckets of tools, garden and kitchen things,
stuffed animals, musical instruments, old jewelry and rings.
Enjoy a donut as you dig through our old clothes,
camping equipment, roller skates and dress shoes.
Haggle us down to a dollar a bag -- everything goes!
No reasonable or even ridiculous offer will be refused.
We're tired of looking at all of it, that's all we know.

SITTING ON THE FRONT STEPS WATCHING THE MOON

Mid June, or mid August, or sometime in May,
not that it matters, except that the weather is warm enough
for short-sleeves, shorts and sandals, and the trees
are in full leaf, framing the quiet street where
as you look out the front door without thinking
you are suddenly struck by the luminous
disc of the full moon rising over the roof of the
abandoned hospital, illuminating the asphalt, the shingles
of neighboring houses, tree-limbs, this glowing face
of an old friend returned from a journey to share
a quiet conversation in the warm evening air,
as you sit down on the front steps in rapt
attention, arms wrapped around legs
and no other thoughts beyond watching and being there.

BREAKFAST AT ELMER'S

A "clean, well-lighted place" in the early morning.
Driving or walking past on the way to work,
especially in winter, in cold darkness,
I longed to stop for a coffee and scrambled eggs,
for hash-browns crisp and two strips of bacon,
to fortify myself for the coming day
and watch the world pass by from a window booth
as if I had "world enough and time."
But, like the other poet, I had "miles to go,"
and nothing to spare to share breakfast with a friend.

When I was teaching at ISU, we came in mid-morning,
after the eight and nine o'clock lectures to
sleepy faces. Three or four of us,
colleagues in arms, crossing the street
to air out our troubles over strawberry Belgian waffles.
Later, in mid-career, I got up early
for Men's Bible Study with omelets or blue-berry pancakes
in the front room with the electric fireplace,
before facing customer meetings and chinese fire drills.

Things are different now that I'm retired.
I come at a decent hour for a breakfast with friends,
either walking, or riding my bike, or with the car
if I am late or lazy or have other errands.
Sometimes Jane and I will stop in after shopping
or touring garage sales on Saturday,
after the urgent early crowds have cleared out.
We sit in the back room over coffee and crepes,
trying to remember the things we were planning to do
or maybe deciding we have already done enough
and watching the folks who pass by
is our new favorite game.
You can see this retirement life is pretty rough.

Things always change, but Elmer's is still the same.

ALMOST POLYGAMY

The people who I worship with
know nothing of my poetry.
The people who I work among
know nothing of my piety.
The friends I read my poems for
know neither work nor church,
and those I play stringed music with,
        (singing for all I'm worth),
know nothing of my other separate lives.

It is as if I had four different wives
and lived at different hours in different houses,
trying to be an honest, faithful man
        (deliberately deceiving none of them)
to all my different spouses.

FOR THE OLD COMPANION

Being gentle at last with my body,
Having driven it unmercifully for years,
Not caring what I poured down its throat, into its lungs
Or drove its feet through as if on some military campaign,
Plunging headlong into each day without breakfast,
A quick cup of coffee, a banana lasting till noon and
Staying up all hours of the night writing poems, drinking
Vintage wines and cognac and espresso into the early hours.
I now turn away from all that, gouty, tender in all parts, decide
To take care of this faithful companion, give it some rest,
More water, more vegetables, whole grains, broiled fish, time
To reflect during long walks on the flat paths of the graveyard
At noon on our lunch hour, looking for a spot to rest,
I say to it, relax, take it easy, walk slowly, last a long time.

THE MAPLE WOOD HAT

Bob Lipp has carved himself a cowboy hat
Out of a fifty-five pound block of maple wood.
Bob, who for his living works as an engineer,
Turns hardwood into artwork on a laser lathe
To keep his soul alive. It took at least forty
Hours (but who's counting?) to realize his
Design, now finished and varnished and
Looking for all the world like a custom
Straw Stetson, gambler style, except
Up close suddenly you see the grain
And say 'Whoa, Bob -- whatchu got there?'
Astounded by the workmanship, folks always
Ask 'How'd you do it?' instead of the
More obvious question -- 'Why?'
To which Bob only smiles and puts the hat
Back on his head, because like true love,
Art and passion cannot be explained
But only served.
`   And Bob?
It goes without saying, of course.
Having finished the hat,
He's working on the horse.

A WINDOWSILL OF POEMS

Poems germinate like dark winter dreams
or tomato seeds in small plastic cups
set on a windowsill in February.
They absorb increasing light day by day,
Nurture, nurture the first green flags
that portend thick vines lopping over baskets,
tomatoes like fresh, plump trollops, saucy and ripe,
the smooth flesh, tiny seeds, acidic bursts
of tart juice spicing the tongue when bit into like an apple,
or simmered into sauce with garlic and sliced peppers.
Our summer depends on green tomatoes slips
absorbing winter light on a windowsill,
As our lives depend on young poems reaching up,
like sonnets unfolding their green wings while we sleep.

MOCHA JAVA JAM

Gimme your sweet java, baby,
Serve your crankin' jo,
Fill my cup with mocha, mama
Till it overflow.
Love your steamy latte, lady,
Love your milky brown;
Froth frangelic frappacino,
Let me drink it down.
Grind, yes grind your strong espresso
Urgent, hot and thick,
Whip me orange frangipano
With a cinnamon stick.
You're my cuppa cappuccino,
Eyes as black as beans.
I'm your macho macchiato,
Moustache full of crème.
Come, my smokin' sweet Barista,
Put the 'mo in my jo,
And wrap your lovely mind around
My sexual innuendo.

THE PAINTER IN THE NIGHT

I would see him always after dark
As I walked home from the library --
The door of the garage thrown open
To the autumn weather, a bright bulb
Splashing white light on the large canvas
And him before it, slashing black lines
Across a yellow field, blue bursts on red blotches,
Completely oblivious to any passerby.

By day he worked at the factory outside town.
By night he painted whatever he damn well pleased.
I thought it was a fantastic way to live.

He had a one-man show down in Columbus.
Driving home, he was hit head-on
By a semi-tractor trailer and was dead.
He left a big yellow canvas inside my head.

"ONE OF THE ROUGHS"

Let me hang out with the roughs,
off on the fringe, away from the seminar room,
the lecture hall and other official gatherings of *literati*.

Give me the company of those with mud on their boots,
holes in their jeans and rough, calloused hands,
matching the style of their poems.

The Muse rides us hard
and toughens our words and our attitudes.
She takes us to places polite people don't want to go.

Driven to the knife-edge, desperate, hungry and sore,
we throw all our words to the whirlwind,
and don't give a damn.

She's one tough bitch to keep happy, whatever we do.
But we live and die in her service, dead-honest and true.

NUMBER 5 JUNE BUG HOPPER

Sometimes I like to tie up a special poem
to attract that elusive aficionado who waits on the bottom
like a monster brown trout at the back of the audience.

I go through all my patterns until I find
a wet fly that's irresistible if delivered right,
with a gentle flick of the wrist across the stream of faces.

I'll start with a burst of color to get attention,
a slightly scandalous image screened over by fox fur
and run on a patter of dactyls with a smattering of rhyme,

add a fringe of hot pink for a lurid look,
a deep image confounded by the iridescence of peacock tail,
and three quivering quills of irony to hide the hook.

That should make old Methuselah jump and squirm.
For everyone else, I normally just use worms.

13 WAYS OF LOOKING AT A WOMAN WITH CROCODILES

Jerusalem AP, March 26, 2007 – A woman with three crocodiles strapped to her waist was stopped at the Gaza-Egypt border after guards noticed that she looked 'strangely fat.' . . . A body search by a female border guard turned up the animals, each about 20 inches long, concealed underneath her loose robe. . . The policewoman screamed and ran out of the room . . . but when the hysteria died down everyone was admiring a woman who is able to tie crocodiles to her body."

1.

When asked why she had three crocodiles strapped to her body,
the Palestinian woman told the border guards that she was
bringing them into Gaza.

"They need more crocodiles," she said.

2.

Bringing crocodiles into Gaza
Is like bringing sharks into Las Vegas.

3.

The female border guard ran screaming from the room.

"I thought it was explosives under her dress," she cried,
"but no, it was crocodiles!"

4.

I sympathize,
I, who have crossed many a border
With crocodiles strapped to my ass.

5.

Who among us cannot but admire
This fashion princess of the runway aisles,
This model of mid-east haut-couture,
This woman strung with living crocodiles.

6.

A woman and Gaza are one.
A woman and Gaza and three crocodiles are one.

7.

Politics is a desperate tango
Danced in a garden of crocodiles.

8.

We walk to work in crocodile shoes,
Singin' those low-down crocodile blues.

9.

The White House Rose Garden blooms
With microphones and crocodiles.

10.

so much depends
upon

three croco-
diles

eating white
chickens

beside the wheel
barrow

11.

In the dark night of the soul,
The only thing moving
was the eye of a crocodile.

12.

So many.
I had not thought
Crocodiles had undone so many.

13.

Then I laughed till I fell out of my shoes --
The sorry day redeemed by crocodile news.

SINGING IN THE SLIPSTREAM

I go out singing
Into the slipstream air of a
Summer twilight sky with steel and lemon light on the mountains
Wind rushing in the driver's side window as I speed along
Singing what comes to mind without caring if it is right or wrong
We go into the night air, my song and I, as the car speeds down the
Canyon curves like a hand frisking the firm flank of a willing dancer and we
Dance together, the sinuous night and I, her eyes full of wander-lust
And a promise given only to me this evening as she tongues it
Like wind in my ear in my shirt the syllables of song
You are the one, the only one, you are
The only one for me.

NIGHT SOFTBALL AT THE WATERWORKS

I must have been twelve when we went there,
two buddies and I, cruising small town streets after dark.
We ventured across the railroad tracks and the river bridge
to the south side of town where the houses were poor
and the tough kids hung out, cat-calling and smoking cigarettes.
Down a broken street and a dirt alley was the ballpark,
built beside the old brick waterworks. Bright lights on poles
illuminated the field where men in their twenties played
fast-pitch softball for a raucous crowd that jeered and cheered them on.
We leaned with our bikes on the fence and drank creme soda.
Men and women drank beer in the stands and smoked.
The eyes of the women glittered and their lipstick was red.
We were eager, excited, but didn't know what to do next.
Half an hour later we snuck out and rode home to bed.

LUNCH AT BUDDY'S

Best to arrive late most days, say
around one-thirty or two, after the crowd,
when the place clears out a bit and you can have
some space by the window in the bar or
along the back wall in the family area because
the stone floors magnify all the voices
and with waiters scurrying past you carrying
trays of salad and the large pizzas
or buss-boys clearing up with a clatter of dishes
it can be hard to have intense conversation,
which is what lunch at Buddy's is best for
along with the heaped-up garlic salad,
so much you can't believe it and
no one can scoop it into the bowls without
spilling garlicky leaves onto the table,
and of course the pizza, always the best in town,
and the sandwiches, spaghetti, ravioli made
with the same red sauce, recipe unchanged since
they opened in the '60's -- if you came then
and came back now it would taste exactly
the same -- which is the genius of this
hole-in-the-wall one-of-a-kind not-
to-be-duplicated accept-no-substitutes
center of the culinary universe in Pocatello,
where you can sit all afternoon nursing
your second beer or a glass of simple Chianti
or one of those exotic cream-topped Italian sodas
with your best friend, your brother who you
haven't seen in years, the whole crazy
family or soccer team or a table of
complete strangers laughing together as if
you had all the time in the world,
which you do, at Buddy's --
you really do.

FLOATING ON MY BACK

July afternoon in Las Vegas, sinfully hot.

I am floating on my back on a mesh raft
        in the modest backyard pool where my son lives.

My granddaughter, just thirteen, a leggy gazelle
        with mischief in her eyes, floats on a raft beside me.

She has a squirt-gun and I have a squirt-gun, filled and ready,
        while we float quietly around, bumping gently.

Five summers ago, in the city pool in Pocatello,
        I taught her to float on her back.

It is the most difficult skill one can teach another --
        to relax and lie back in the water, held up by another's hands.

Once she caught on, she was floating all around the lazy river
        like a buoyant cork, confident and joyous.

Sometimes we floated around together, side by side,
        her slim arm resting on my wrist like a tether.

It is something we share, this floating and looking up,
        trusting each other to be calm and still.

Then she rolls off and blasts me a good one in the face.

TRUCKS IN MY DREAMS ALL NIGHT

When we lived in that house on Detroit Street
trucks drove past our block all night,
downshifting, braking, shifting gears, revving up,
throbbing their engines at the traffic light,
and although it got so I didn't hear them at all,
sometimes, waking up in the dark room,
they seemed like the guardians of my dreams,
vigilant, growling, scaring the bedside monsters,
so I could curl back under covers, safe and tight,
while big wheeled trucks roared through my sleep all night.

SWINGING FROM THE TREETOP LIKE A TROMBONE

I grew up playing Glenn Miller and Tommy Dorsey swing in high school band --
Moonlight Serenade, Chattanooga ChooChoo, A-Train and all those WWII tunes
My father's generation swung to swung as well in my braincells.
Last night we attended an ABBA tribute concert, surrounded mostly by gray hairs like me,
Waving their arms in the air and clapping to *Dancing Queen*, but also some
Younger families, my kid's age, with their young children, dancing in the aisles.
Consciousness overlaps generations. These kids will probably not dig Dorsey,
But they dig ABBA. I, who learned Dorsey as they are learning ABBA, bridge the gap
Between my father's generation and my grandchildren's, who will have their own heroes
I have not heard and cannot imagine liking or understanding the way they will,
So that on the far end of my life I once more confront strange tunes that belong to others,
While rooted in the middle, the music of the sixties and seventies looms like a large,
sheltering tree with so many branches, Dylan, Hendricks, Cash, Haggard, Beach Boys,
Elvis, Flat & Scruggs, Beatles, Stones, Mamas & Papas, Everly Brothers, Hank and even
ABBA spreading cool shade across consciousness from Goodman to Gilkyson, a bridge
Touching the front-end of my grandchildren's musical imagination like fingertips
Passing what torches they wish to pick up so that it rolls along like the City of New Orleans
Into the new morning I cannot see but feel already coming toward us at great speed.

THANKSGIVING SURPRISE

Dad had just finished carving the steaming turkey as in that
Norman Rockwell painting with Mom and us kids and Grandma
and maybe old Mrs. Kelly and Doctor Combs around the dining room table
when from the backyard came a sudden crash like a bomb going off
and we all got up and looked out the window while Dad and
Doctor Combs went down the back steps to see where
our neighbor, old man Stewart, drove his Buick
through the back brick wall of his garage.

That was one Thanksgiving Rockwell never painted!

EMAIL TO myfolks@paradise.com

Dear Mom and Dad,

This morning I had this desire to send you an email,
so casual, as I sip morning coffee, snow falling gently outside
and thirty to fifty years since we last spoke to each other.
It seemed the most natural thing to do somehow
as if electronic media, like prayer, was capable
of crossing the space-time continuum back to
some morning in 1955 to catch us all at
breakfast, eating our Creme-of-Wheat
around the kitchen table, before
the day began, just to say
I still remember you
as you were so many years ago,
strong, vigorous in your mid-life activities,
raising a house full of children, cooking meals,
walking to the downtown office to do everyone's income tax
and sliding thoughtlessly through an ordinary morning,
snow falling perhaps, or light spring rains,
the fresh air wafting window screens
with no thought of tomorrow let
alone the end of the century
and this weird decade
of incredible technologies
with the same old problems in the world
and your grown, retired son, gray-bearded, bald,
sitting at a desk, drinking souped-up coffee and keyboarding
some electronic message on a gleaming screen that
highlights my spelling errors but not my
unspoken love for you, for those
days, that time, lost beyond
photographs to which my
email cannot be delivered as addressed but
will come bouncing back breaking
in some profound way
this heart that
after all these years still
loves you
more than I can say.
Be well :)

Harald

CHAMPAGNE AT THE TOP OF THE WORLD

This bright table set with heavy silver in the midday sun,
crisp white tablecloth, vase of flowers, starched napkins
and wide windows open to the harbor and Lake Michigan
where last evening we cruised in a tour boat from the pier
to see the Chicago skyline as the sun went down;
now here, in the Signature Room on the 95th floor,
observing, this glorious midday, as if from heaven itself
the peaceful pace of everyday life humming below
and our son and his daughter, Sierra, our delight,
watching across the table as we pause and lift
two crystal flutes of sparkling white wine from France,
touch them gently together, smile at each other and taste
the effervescent fortune of our forty-three years --
so lucky (so lucky!) surrounded in sunlight -- to be here!

FOR DONALD JOLLIFF

On his eightieth birthday

Of farmhouse, field, forest, family and farm;
of caring for living things and loving friends;
of corn and wheat, oats, alfalfa and soybeans;
of uncut woodland, bramble, maple, oak, hickory, beech;
of songbirds and nesters, bluebirds, robins and wrens --
a small box on every fencepost, welcoming them --
of such perfect things, a man comprehends his life.

Of parents remembered and long ancestral bloodlines
and brothers and sisters with all their marvelous progeny;
of your partner especially, best friend, lover and wife,
and greenhouse hothouse flowers to be given away,
and kitchen dominion of piecrusts, pot roasts, preserves --
the mind scrap-booking a lifetime held vivid and warm
of farmhouse, field, forest, family and farm.

DINNER AT OLIVER'S

Often, on Friday nights in the late '90's, those middle years
when we were still employed, but after the children had grown,
before so many good friends retired and moved away,
we would gather in the back room of Oliver's Restaurant,
pull several tables together to seat six or eight couples,
and spend two or three hours with a leisurely dinner together
as if in a Trattoria or Gasthaus in Europe where you stay as long as you like,
rather than the fashion in most American commercial grills where you
eat and move on to make room for the crowd at the door.

At Oliver's, on Friday nights, there was no crowd at the door
(unlike Saturday mornings when you can't find an empty spot).
The backroom was capacious, welcoming and often deserted,
no strangers to offend with our garrulous, loud conversation,
and the food was good, solid, predictable American fare --
spaghetti and meatballs, pork chops with green beans, lasagna,
chicken-fried steak, prime rib with baked potato, sensible salads --
all reasonably priced for "Seniors". We were invited to bring
our own bottle(s) of wine -- no corking fee required, though
we often brought our own corkscrews and even some
crystal from home if they ran out of glasses. Quite often
the value in vintage wines exceeded the price of the meals.

Here we would gather, good friends in our fifties and sixties,
(in the prosperous last years of the Clinton Presidency,
between the gulf wars, that interlude of relative peace)
and dine at our leisure for hours, drinking Bordeaux
and regaling each other with the little news of our lives,
some scandalous jokes, some gossip of churches or neighbors,
or even, at times, passionate political rants, philosophic debates,
theological diatribes, scientific discourses or quiet discussions
about children or problems with siblings or bosses, the stresses
of work, frustrations with government, whatever rose up in the heart.
We were all so different in background, degrees, professions, faiths
(or lack thereof), political leanings, childhood backgrounds, exiles all,
gathered from different states of the union to this small western town,
yet for all that, similar in age, children of parents who had lived through
the 30's and fought in the 40's and knew the value of a dollar and a promise,
all of us come of age under Kennedy and Johnson, in the Vietnam years,
tempered enough by turmoil to appreciate the solace of relative
peace and prosperity, blessings of health, children all safely raised
and the joy of a few hours together on a Friday night in a quiet back room
with passable food and excellent wine at the end of a week's adventures
where we finished our pie a'la mode and decaf coffee amid
warm conversation before passing out into the deep starry night,

to re-enter our whirlpool, whitewater lives refreshed and upheld
by friendship that passes too quickly, except out of memory,
and is not to be met with again this side of hereafter,
when we may yet have the good fortune to gather
once more around some capacious welcoming table,
where the friendship is sparkling and the stories unending --
some perfected, heavenly Oliver's in the sky.

AUTUMN SMOKE

When I was nine or ten, we played
Touch football after supper every night
Until it go too dark to see the ball in the trees,
The air smoky with the smell of burning leaves,
The grass cold and dew-damp when you fell on it,
My friends all yelling in the brushed gold afterglow
Beneath the maples dropping their bits of orange and red
On lawns of white frame houses across the street,
The cold night air, October in the park,
And us riding our bikes home just before dark.

THE PICKLE PATCH

Thinking back on it now, it must have been
somewhat like the lost family castle in Cockermouth
that Dad visited while in England during the war.
A dirt road led through fields and across a rickety bridge
to a copse of trees over-grown and falling over
that surrounded a ruined farmhouse with broken windows
where no one had lived since the Great Depression.
We ate our picnic at an mossy old table.
I pumped the pump handle but got no water to rise,
Mother picked a kerchief full of raspberries
and my sister climbed on a pile of old, decrepit logs.
Only Dad remembered when the house was lit up and alive
with aunts and uncles, cousins and big barking dogs.

BRINGING IN THE SPUDS

We drove the VW bus out into the field,
across furrows, following the packed-down tracks
of huge potato trucks that carried the harvest off days ago,
parked in the midst of a thousand acres of grit,
the sandy loam you scrub off an Idaho russet
before baking them for dinner. The kids got out
and we took our cardboard boxes from row to row
looking for random potatoes scattered about,
the ones the digger missed or sorted out,
some small as tennis balls, others big as footballs,
some distorted, with noses, ears and weird protuberances.

We packed boxes to overflowing and lugged them to the bus
until, at last, we had a load. The sun had already set
and the harvest moon, masked in orange smoke,
hung in a burgundy haze on the blue horizon.
We felt rich as kings with our treasure -- free potatoes! --
gleaned from the soil by hand in the crisp evening air!
Drove back past fields where diggers with their headlights on
did their dusty business in the dark, getting
the harvest in before frost, finishing
the seasonal cycle on the land --
bringing in the spuds.

We got home hungry and tired and
washed four of the largest ones for dinner.
Baked and buttered, nothing in the world tasted better.

THE YOUNG REBEL

One thing he knew --
He would not do
What others wanted him to do --
And that was his undoing.

SIERRA IN A STRAW HAT

Says she hates it -- this straw hat
With twisted brim bent down the front and back
And cord to catch on her chin when the wind blows it off.

Has no concept how cute she looks in it --
"the kid" -- skinny minny, long stick legs, sunskirt and top --
hair in beaded island braids that bang back and forth
as she rides her bike on the driveway in the sun,
and squirts the orange day lilies with the hose,
and makes chalk drawings, sporting a secret smile.

Eight years old -- spunky-dainty -- a 'tom boy' and a 'girly girl,'
Charged with energy for helping, watering, biking, hiking, painting
the wheel barrow with flowers and butterflies, swinging higher and higher.

Freckled nose, large deep eyes, the glaring grin mischievous
Beneath the bent straw brim as she poses impatiently for the photograph.

DUTCHER'S MEAT MARKET

The oak wood floor was slippery with sawdust
as we walked down the aisles of canned goods
to the porcelain and glass counter in the back
where the enormous black horns of a steer
hung over the mustached face of the butcher
who grinned at us as he sharpened his knife
and cut through a hanging side of red meat
to lay three slabs on the tray of the scales
and wrap them up in white paper tied with string.
Before we walked out, the butcher winked at my Dad
and sliced off two slivers of sausage, for him and for me.

THE WANDERING BOOKS

I made a great discovery yesterday
in the used book section of St. Vincent de Paul
while my wife was looking at second-hand sweaters.
It was a New and Collected Poems by a famous writer
I have always been meaning to read, a guy
who is published regularly in American Poetry Review
and other top notch literary mags
so there must be something to his stuff
although I probably wouldn't pay retail to find out --
and here it was -- in prefect condition -- for a dollar-fifty!
I don't think it had been opened except one time
when the author inscribed his name, fifteen years ago,
so it must have been bought after a reading
and never looked at since. How it waited
like a virgin bride in a convent, locked
in tight ranks on an academic's bookshelf until
in some moment of disorder and impersonal parsing
(not unlike the separation of weak from strong at Auschwitz)
it was sent to the left without a second thought,
donated to charity, the bottom of the market, one step away
from the landfill or the pulping mill, given a new chance
to find a reader, someone like me, mildly curious,
friendly, if uncommitted, willing to choose,
since the price was more than fair
and the risk minimal, adding it
to the congregation of unread books
on my nightstand (safe harbor, temporary shelter
from the storm-troopers), and even to read
a poem or two, at least, just to taste
and perhaps find here what I have been looking for.

The selection is careful and callous, be it books
or apples in the grocery or those we love,
perceived across a room, sought after,
courted with earnest guile, pursued
to the altar and lived with even for a lifetime,
in the best cases, opened, tasted, held to the heart,
the pearl of great price for which all is given,
or, as so often happens, not opened,
abandoned, discarded, a mistake
as the heart looks further for that special one
to fit our fickle dreams.
So we pray for our children
and grandchildren, that they may choose
and be chosen by someone who wants them

124

above all others, and they as well,
so all of their pages are opened, bent back and read
and nothing is left unspoken or unloved.
And, for writers, that hope extends to our books.

Later in the day we stopped at the library
to return two books on tape -- one we had listened to
driving across two states, gripped so intently by tension
that I had to turn it off in city traffic -- the other,
less compelling for some reason, although well written,
was just not what we wanted -- so it goes.
As we scanned the shelves up front, where the library
sells books that have been donated by patrons
or just not chosen often enough from the stacks, I found --
of all things! -- a book of my poems --
published twenty years ago at great expense,
the most ambitious project I've ever attempted
and still a personal favorite -- on the rack,
priced at $1.00, in good condition,
though not inscribed, perhaps
the library copy, unread all these years,
pulled to give limited shelf-space to another,
and set on the side of the tracks to be chosen, or not,
headed toward someone's reading stack
or onto the streets, my forlorn child.

I was tempted to buy it, out of love or vanity,
but then I put it back, hoping still
in the random shuffling of minds and hearts
all looking for something they are scarcely aware of seeking,
that one special soul might come -- the writer's dream --
who has been looking high and low for --
THIS BOOK, THIS ONE, YOU! OH MY GOD! --
out of all the crowd of faces on the rack --
to take home, to read cover to cover, slowly, lingering,
to put in a place of honor by the bedside,
touching the pages, finding the truth
crafted through art and intention,
which they have been seeking all their life --
the pearl of great price, the rock
in the temple mount, the
Chosen One. Maybe.

I think about Whitman's spider, sending out "filament, filament . . ."
until something sticks, and all the hopeful books with their
sensuous come-hither covers in so many languages, wandering the world,
standing on platforms, auction blocks, in back-street windows,
book-seller's stalls along the Seine or the Thames or in

famous bookstores -- Gotham, Powell's, City Lights --
carried on the backs of peddlers to book fairs in Frankfurt
or small towns in Iowa, blowing like dandelion fluff across prairies
or crowded like the parable seed onto a bookshelf of thistles,
crammed in the back with the well used "working books,"
bent over backward, dog-eared, folded, smudged, discarded at last
in places where no one would pay even a nickel to free them from bondage,
their only hope Heaven, that ultimate library, where each book
is honored and the angels know them by heart.

But that is unlikely, given what we know
about natural selection and the fate of all living things.
The faceless millions are ground down like shells on the seashore
or mulch for the fields, "good manure" to quote Walter again,
and only a few lifted up into the light. C'est la vie.
As for the New and Collected Poems,
It's down in the stack, third in line.
I might get to it in a week or two, who knows?
Or then I might just take it
to Good Will.

AT THE BOOKFAIR

The books sit in their Sunday clothes
like girls on folding chairs against the wall
of the Junior High gymnasium at a dance.
The readers wander by, shy, tentative,
like thirteen-year-old boys in awkward suits.
The music plays and plays in vain for hours;
the mirrored globe spins diamonds around the floor;
but nobody is dancing. The friendly books
smile and cast inviting looks at eyes
that glance and almost engage, then look away
as the saxophone plays its most sorrowful swansong
and all the books are thinking: *"Come on! Come on!*
Choose me -- choose anyone -- but DANCE!
Before the last song dies away -- it's your last chance!"

FORTY-SEVENTH ANNIVERSARY

Rising before sunrise, in shorts, sweatshirt and sandals I venture out
to start the sprinklers, fill the bird feeders, move gently about
carry watering cans to the outlying flowerbeds and pots,
pull a few weeds in the garden, swing to and fro
and listen to the meadowlark on his fencepost perch
serenade the brightening morning like Caruso.

You sleep in this purple hour, moon in the western sky,
cool wind from the mountain filling your window with birdsong.
I spray the perennials -- iris, columbine, peony, red rose, syringa --
moistening their sensuous petals with dripping wet silver,
as the sun breaks like a welding torch in the northeast notch,
engorging the hips of the hayfields with emerald fire.

You smile at the window, serene in a sunlit space,
the beautiful world reflected in your face.

GIN RUMMY BY CANDLELIGHT

Jane and I, snowfall, the power outage lasting all afternoon
and into the darkness of a chilly Sunday evening,
lit candles in kitchen and dining room,
and, since there was no way to fix dinner,
sat in their flickering luminescence
(red and white and yellow and green candles
in cut glass holders, bowls and mason jars
wavering their sinuous warm flames)
with a flexible deck of Bicycle playing cards,
shuffling and dealing hand after hand of
gin rummy, as in the early days of our marriage
in that small upstairs apartment on Summit Street,
our daughter asleep in her crib, we played
to a thousand, secure in love's solitude and soft remarks.

CRUISING THE FARMER'S MARKET

A Saturday morning in late July,
temps in the eighties, hot sun, blue sky,
the smell of warm air baking off the concrete
and friendly blue-grass music in the air
as you and your sweetie (and perhaps your dog)
saunter arm in arm in a roil of casual strollers,
looking for carrots and kale, fresh beets, green beans
and that newly picked sweet corn and the first tomatoes
not grown in a hot-house -- bite into one and suck the tart juice,
letting some of it dribble down your chin and onto your t-shirt like a
sign of complete satisfaction -- SUMMER IS HERE!
Not only farmers but artisans, too -- crafters of all sorts
market their wares from the shade of their shelters --
wood-craft and baked goods and decorated light switch-plates,
lamp-stand structures of glued glass-ware and whimsical sunflowers
welded from farm implements and bicycle chains --
hand-made jewelry, plastic composting tubes and worm farms --
and more than a few folks selling cheeses and sausages,
artisan breads, sticky buns and organic bionic vegan smoothies --
treats for your pets and do-it-yourself garden planters --
there's even a guy who will give you a massage or
perhaps tell your fortune or sell you portions
of grass-fed beef or free-range lambs.
Whatever you're craving there's somebody catering,
and even if you're not in the mood or the market
of left your money at home or came here
by accident -- wandering costs nothing
and what else would you do
with warm temps, hot sun and blue sky
this Saturday morning in Idaho late in July?

THE FROGS IN THE PICKLE JAR

It seemed so scientific,
catching tree-frogs,
creating an environment --
twigs, dead grass, lid full of water --
all inside a large pickle jar
with a cheese-cloth cover for ventilation.
We were fascinated watching them for hours.

After three days Mom pitched it all out with the trash.

SELF IMPROVEMENT 101

I am a lucky man to have such friends
who have nothing else to do but to attend
to all the failings with which my life is fraught
and diligently teach what can't be taught.

In vain I beg them not to be so kind.
They are determined to improve my mind.
My posture's bad, they say -- I am too fat --
and as for pride, I am the prince of that.

And yet, although their warm solicitude
is intended solely for my good,
I would rather roast in Purgatory
than change one inch of personality.

And since each sinner's cross remains his own,
why can't the perfect leave the damned alone?

STEPPING AWAY FROM IT ALL

When this corporeal collection of stardust disappears
and consciousness transforms beyond imagining,
what was myself will merge with all that is,
accompanied by myriad other beings around the world
who pass beyond all caring on that day --
the rich and famous few, the unknown many,
great and small, the starving, wretched poor,
infants, refugees, abandoned, neglected, abused,
victims of murder and of unending war,
whose names are only known to the Great Unknown --
on equal footing we step out together
into the greater stream of shining souls,
joyously gathered back to beginnings again,
one body, one being, one mystery, life without end.

WALKING AROUND TOWN

The nice thing about being retired
is you have a lot of time to walk around.
The nice thing about Pocatello
is there are endless neighborhoods to wander in.
Summer mornings or late afternoons
when everyone else is sleeping or working
the streets and sidewalks are empty and full of shade.
I often hike up through the University,
sometimes climbing to the columns on Red Hill,
then meander across campus casually,
waiting till classes have changed and things are still,
then dive down one of the avenues,
turning at every block to change the pattern,
stopping perhaps for a cup of gourmet coffee
or to shoot the breeze with an old friend on their porch
before arriving eventually at my home.

I love the character of each city block,
the varying styles of houses on each side of the street,
some high and mighty, boasting architecture,
others cookie cutter images of each other
and yet for that, no two are really alike
as income, attitude, resources and personal taste
reflect each owner's personality --
the outside facade resembling the folks within,
as what we are results in how we live.
In any given block you will find
modest dwellings kept up neat as a pin
with recent paint jobs and the yard full of flowers,
flanked on one side by a neglected rental
and on the other by a roofed basement
which nevertheless has marigolds in each window.
Some folks keep their lawns immaculate,
while others replace the grass with stones and shrubs.
In some front yards chickens wander about,
pecking their breakfast beneath the sunflower stalks;
in others are planters of onions, tomatoes, peppers and beans.
No matter. New wonders arise at every turn.

The only thing better than mornings or afternoons
walking these funky neighborhoods for hours,
is to have dinner with a friend at Oliver's or Buddy's
and then stroll through darkening streets by the light of the moon.

CLIMBING

MOUNT BONNEVILLE

CLIMBING MOUNT BONNEVILLE

We park at the ski lodge at first light
And hike the cat tracks up for two hours straight
As sunlight works its way across the valley
And canyon winds scour the tall fir trees.

My buddy and I make our first ascent.
He knows the trails from winter skiing.
We stride on broken rocks, a few beer cans,
Lost ski poles, human debris. Early August.

The last half hour after the cat tracks end
We scramble the rocky watershed straight up,
Skirting the palisade to the right,
Cresting the stony saddle into sunlight.

On top! Nothing above us but blue!
And the wind rushing at us up the mountain,
Indian paintbrush, blue lupine, fuscia lover's star,
And the world sun-struck in all directions.

On all sides, a meadow of late summer flowers
blooming for our solitary pleasure.
You sense ancestral spirits walking here.
We sit on a flat outcrop and eat our sandwiches.

The soul expands like a sail to fill the sky
And the heart, unable to contain itself, sings out --
Freedom! Freedom! If Heaven is anywhere,
It cannot be more perfect than this place.

Part of me will climb down in an hour.
Part of me will stay up here forever. When I die,
my soul will ride high thermals like a hawk
Into this meadow -- never come down again.

IMMORTALITY

The tall dry grass beside the road
With heavy straw-colored seeds that nod in the wind
And lean together, tangled and top-heavy,
Beyond them, the mountain range across the valley
The color of plums on the top ridge in the new sunrise,
The aspen grove ahead, still in cool shadow
Where the road turns to the left and begins to climb
Elevating the heart-rate as you stride without stopping
Until cresting you look at the manicured fields
Where only last week they took off the winter wheat.
The feminine contours of the countryside,
The deep ravines full of wild brush,
Where the resident hawk soars on tipped wings
Announcing his liftoff with a primal 'skree'!
The quakies are already yellowing at the edges
And chokecherries are black and ruby amid the green.
In meadows of hip-deep rust-colored grass,
The road leads straight over hills out of eyesight --
No one for miles, no farmhouse, no sound
Save the scritch of my boots on gravel.
I saunter and stroll farther and farther away
From everything that holds me, entering a place
I can never be called back from and never forsake.
Though my body be less than a clod of dirt in the field,
My soul lifts off on strong speckled wings into space.

NESTOR'S WOODS

January

To the spinning deceptions of the inner world --
anxieties striking strings through a madman's concerto,
worries chattering their monkey voices up to no good --
this counterpoint: the stand of aspen trees in Nestor's Woods.

Snowfall slows me down. My old boots leave perfect prints
on the soft roadside. And in the tangled grove, half-hidden in fog,
tree limbs, branches, red willows, tall thistle crowns, lank bitter-bush
are cold-crusted with inch-thick hoarfrost delicate as lace.

I lean on the stick to catch the breath that wreathes
around my face and frosts my beard. Flickering between limbs,
a small bird draws my eye, then disappears. It is so cold,
the inner gears synch up with the outer wheels.

There is one breath, one vision and one place.
Beyond the human, this is how life feels.

February

They stand like Rodin's *Burghers of Calais,*
This chorus of tall aspens rooted in the ravine.
An owl's nest makes a mouth like Munch's *The Scream*
as overhead bare branches shiver and sway.

Had they legs, they'd be knee deep in snow,
old and crusted and shrunken by cold rains
that came a month too soon, bursting the domain
of winter with a scud of storms that bluster and blow

no good to frozen fields or the man on foot,
who shields eyes and ears against the blast,
pausing only a moment to confront these oracles,
who witness whatever comes and let it pass.

The Beautiful stands hidden within her gates.
All things come in time to him who waits.

March

Walk in the evening sunlight, soft and warm,
the dirt road leading you gently up and around,
and on the ridgeline, outlined against pale blue
the crowns of aspens clotted with burst buds.

There is no wind tonight -- the empty sky
spreads its backdrop behind the spreading trees,
and here, in the hollow, red stems hide the stream,
and there, thick clumps of grass fold over the ravine,
like ancient hair protecting the vulnerable gash.

All nature hovers, hesitant, in the blocks,
awaiting the starter's gun to spring suddenly forth.
Red spears of new grass poke through decayed leaves.
A small bird enters the branches and then sits still.

The dirty snow-bank melts in the crotch of the hill.

April

The grove commits to green, each tree aflame
with new leaves incandescent in the sun,
while in the harrowed fields, still wet and brown,
the blades of spring wheat spear up from the ground,
just barely visible: green hair on the hill's round hump.

I plod the road, still dressed for winter winds
in wool beret, neck scarf, soft gloves, sweatshirt and vest,
while my heart looks hopeful at the undressed trees,
shivering in their shimmies of skinny green,
and yearn for sun-bright breezes, fragrant and warm.

I stand in a medieval painting by Cranach the Elder,
Soft winds stirring the new trees and peasants plowing.
I can almost hear the burble of bagpipe and flute,
fresh runoff tumbling down rocks in the ravine.

May

Sunrise fills the warm skies with white light
above the mountain ridgeline, breaking forth
upon the sensuous mounds of the gentle fields,
riffling green-topped eagerly growing wheat.

And in the woods the trees and bushes are eager,
the aspens in full leaf frisked by the breeze
and chokecherry choked with sweet white blooms
and red willow spurting eager tongues of green.

The grasses already break the dry, gray mat
with strong, aggressive spears of flaming emerald,
while in the hidden branches overhead
magpies, grackles and black-birds cackle and call.

Along the curving incline of the road
I stride in shorts and shirtsleeves like a lord.

June

Green rules the earth like a benevolent god,
expansive, aggressive, dominating the broad land.
Along the roadside, meadow-grass grows slender and tall,
the bushes bear leafy limbs and drooping blossoms,
while overhead leaves quiver in limber quakies.
Spring wheat measured in rows knee-deep and green
carpets the contour of fields like deep-pile carpet
and everywhere vigorous new life shakes in the wind.

The road is damp from last night's thunderstorm.
The morning air is rain-fresh, clean and sweet.
A shredded cloudbank clings to the mountain's rim,
behind which spread the rays of approaching sun.
A moose, hidden by bracken, clatters through the ravine.
The walker on the road stands still, best left unseen.

July

It is too hot, even at six a.m.   One relishes the river of cool air
washing down the swale of yellowing wheat, one wraps
the sweat-shirt round the shoulders and carries the hat,
puffing up the road before sunrise -- summer's peak.

In stillness, baffled between heat and cool, the grove of trees
collects itself, anticipating the approaching scorch. Tall, smooth trunks
with their caps of fluttery leaves, stand to their knees in chokecherries
and dense willow-bush, drawing their deep drink from the stream.

The landscape is as pastel as a painting. Residual smoke in the sky
from the fire two ridge-lines south, softens the sunrise with peach-tones,
darkens the peaks across the valley with plum. The rolling wheat,
half gold, half green, and the tall bronzed seed-heads of roadside grass

beg to be captured by plein-aire artists in soft shirts, wide, floppy hats.
The stream trickles *andante cantabile*, before the furnace doors open.

August

A kingdom of dust that coats the bending grass
and films the boots and leaves its taste on the tongue
whenever a vehicle passes in a cloud. No wind.
Particulate hovers like plague in the lambent air.

Across the valley, smoke from a three-day fire
reddens the sky like a bruise above the mountain.
We hold our breath -- hiker, hayfield, chokecherries, aspen trees --
hoping against all hope for the smallest breeze.

The stream long dry and ravine clogged with thistles,
wheat-fields bent and listless, aching for harvest.
Even the hawk on the wing seems nailed to the sky,
soaring the thermals to nowhere, no need to fly.

What we wouldn't give for a good thundershower!
Blind rain battering our bodies for half-an-hour!

September

The season turns to coolness in morning and evening;
light jacket and cap, boots and socks, perhaps even long pants
as cold air streams like water down the swale
before one strides up and above into residual radiance,
the harvested flatlands reflecting late summer sun.

The breezes carry the first clear whiff of snowfall,
tasted like blue steel back on the tongue
when clouds collaborate to cover up the sun,
despite the dust-devils whirling over the fields.
The mountain ridges hold onto their handful of smoke.

Color invades the flutter of aspen leaves,
still green, but tinged on the edges with yellow and brown.
Flickers and magpies scatter through clusters of trees;
red willows shiver the ravine as the sun goes down.

October

First snow on the ridgeline and ice in the road,
melts before mid-day, but the message is clear:
the easy days are done, there's no time to lose.
Let the sheep-herder park his wagon in the upper fields
and five hundred dusty heads graze alfalfa down to the dirt.

The brown leaves tumble like birds when the hard wind blows,
out of the southwest, threatening rain and snow.
Even the sunshine is chilly in late afternoon.
Take a brisk walk for your health and then head home,
picking up beer-cans, water-bottles, fast-food wrappers, glass.

The bare trees lean together with nothing to say.
The green summer gods have departed, along with the hay,
leaving unsolved problems -- a ditch choked with thistles -- behind
for country folks to cope with. Well, we don't mind.

November

Tromp and scuff for two miles till my boot-heels are sore,
beneath steam-roller storm clouds grinding down hard
with wind like a slap on the cheek, stinging and smart,
as I try to remember some things to be thankful for.

My health, of course -- that I can walk freely and shout
my thoughts on inhuman humanity for the winds to not hear --
and the fact that no tragedy touches those I personally hold dear --
should be more than enough, were I honest, to be thankful about.

But no, not at all -- I huff on in my self-righteous funk
as if I knew secret equations to make things right as rain,
when, in fact, all I do really well is to cause people pain
and deny that my smuggest opinions are nothing but junk.

Turn around. Walk back slow. Breathe deep. Stop talking. Be still.
The motionless tree-limbs know more than you ever will.

December

Trudging in fresh deep snow at the end of the day,
near the corner of Nestor's woods where the road curves left,
I wander straight ahead, through the falling flakes,
to where the tree I love stands hidden in the meadow.

Each year, in every season, I seek its shape,
the tallest aspen tree in the meadow, perfect and straight,
whether glorious in green or golden leaves, or now stripped bare
and almost invisible, it never fails to please me standing there.

We stare at the Nameless swirling above and below,
through complexities blurred as a forest bewildered by snow,
while what we seek stands firm, although concealed
by a veil of drifting details and shifting doubts
until we also stand still within it and without

and the pattern behind the blizzard is revealed.

BONNEVILLE ROAD AT DUSK

Half hour after sundown I set out --
My evening walk in the gloaming, pearl-gray light,
Past hayfield stubble and hip-tall grass,
The golden seeded beards on straw dry stalks
And bands of purple cloud in the western sky,
Mount Bonneville still rosy at its peak, but darkening
As hills are darkening in the cool, fresh streams
Of night air rushing down the swales of the hayfields
And crickets creaking their ancient fiddle-songs,
As tiny points of light scatter across the valley,
Where the meadows create new space as they roll away.
The stars are coming out, and a crescent moon
Hides in the east, new risen over the mountain.
The last birds call to each other, seeking shelter.
Miles below, traffic whines on the highway.
The last shred of daylight leaves the sky.
The air is suddenly still. Nothing stirs.

How amazing, just to be standing here.

THE SMALL RAIN DOWN CAN RAIN

Night of rain and day of rain, sluicing the fields,
Nature doing what she will as always,
Beyond our bidding, impassive, solemn, huge.
And the small trees, the long grass, receive her gift.
We also, in our wicker houses, wait, like finches
For seeds to live on, living off each other.
So the forsythia, newly planted, will survive,
And the seven spruces and the hackberry.
All things seen and unseen will enjoy
Their tiny, private lives beyond the reach
Of governments, corporations or world banks.
The alfalfa grows thick, waist-deep, green and strong,
And it is all I can to do keep from breaking out
Into ecstasy, poetry, mantra, prayer and song.

GLORY

Morning in August, the smell of damp, dried grass,
Second growth alfalfa with its purple flowers,
Light pouring through the notch in the ridgeline,
Sunlight, holy sunlight, filling the broad valley,
My feet, in freedom, striding the gravel road,
Sparrows, wrens, meadowlarks, skitter across fields.

This day, this cool mid-summer morning hour,
This life still pouring forth after so many years,
Water over rocks, hidden by grass, beyond words.

The meadow beneath the aspens, thick with grass,
Stems still green beneath lopsided, bearded seed-heads,
and the tall blue flowers of Canadian thistle.

Sunlight breaks the peak like a welder's torch,
flooding my face with
> glory
>> glory
>>> glory

A THREAD OF MELANCHOLY

Late August now, the downside of the year,
cresting the peak of July with its long, hot days and descending
night by lengthening night, through the unassayed gold of summer
into eventual umber, increasing darkness, decay,
the garden burgeoning with vegetables pushed into ripeness,
the California poppies scattered like Spanish doubloons beside the road,
monster zucchini's lurking beneath broad leaves, the cornstalks rattling
announcing the harvest of carrots, beans, beets, onions, potatoes, squash . . .
and then exhaustion, October, the first frost whitening fence rails,
stalks and vines wither and blacken to be chopped up and spread out
over the rough soil cleared off of all crops, made ready for snow,
the compost heap unpacked with the pitchfork and covered with leaves . . .

Oh, now it starts, that downward cycle, darkness, cold and decay . . .
Across the autumnal fields, a twist of smoke, a thread of melancholy.

TWO SONNETS IN LATE SEPTEMBER

Rain -- solid and relentless
out of the west before the sun comes up.
It will persist all day, followed by
frost and snowfall late tonight,
covering the tomato plants, the beans,
the sweet corn still ungathered
and all the garden work not finished
beneath the waning sun and waxing cold --
but let it go. Let snowfall come when it chooses.
Let the dark nights and winter come as well.
We took our summer glory day by day
like the orange poppies bordering the driveway
and all our happiness has been preserved,
like pickled beets in jars of poetry.

~

Snowfall follows, whitening the fields,
deepening on the garden all the night,
covering the undug carrots in their rows
and unpicked corn and broken onion stalks.
Now October comes, the sallow month,
a grinning jack-o-lantern capped with snow,
it's little joke, the first brief touch of winter
to remind us of mortality, how all that's green
blackens and crumbles like skulls of squash,
while deep roots endure like parsnips under the frost
and life, though silent and withdrawn, survives
to give us a second harvest from home-maker's craft
that captured tomatoes and beets in mason jars
and carrots and onions and beans to pour into the broth.

IN THE BLEAK MID-WINTER'S TEETH

Now we suffer the bleak mid-winter's teeth --
not December blizzards, swirling and bright
with Christmas cheer and glowing Christmas lights,
nor January storms pillowing the slopes
with knee-deep drifts of powder skiers crave --
but rather, late February, waking at five
to blow the driveway clean of wind-driven drifts
that rebuilt all the night where cleared before
their hardened, compact, frozen, sculptured shelves
that even in first gear with grinding force
eleven horses scarce can gnaw through inch by inch,
beneath the scattered, stark, unpatterned stars,
relentless gale winds whipping pellets of sleet in your face,
and tulip-bulbs, lavender, day lilies buried under two feet of ice.

SNOWFALL IN ORDINARY TIME

Snowfall overnight and now once more
The white squall presses on us from the west.
The valley disappears as if in smoke
And tiny flakes drift cross the evergreens
As I put on my coat and scarf and gloves,
My insulated boots and stocking cap,
To venture out for my good morning walk
And face the face of winter in the storm.

All traces of past history are erased --
The bird tracks and the dog tracks and the deer --
My own cross-country tracks from yesterday
Are covered now as though they never were,
And I am free to make fresh marks on snow
As if the first whoever cross fields did go.

LIKE ICARUS

O let me plunge from a great height,
Like a sharp-shinned hawk,
Swift as a bullet in the ice cold rush
Of air and cloud against my face
To streak spinning toward the hills
That seem to come no closer until
Suddenly specific trees stand out --
A road -- rooftops spring up, and I
Like Icarus approach the solid world
Daring every second to smash me flat
Upon a point of rock, until, with miraculous
Ease and incredible speed I spread the
Magnificent red and yellow wings held tight
Against my side during the descent
And soar like a winged god out of annihilation
To glide clean and beautiful over the long grass.

THE POET

In a meadow of tall grass, one aspen tree,
Separate from all others, full-bodied and tall,
Commands the space with quiet majesty.

Each season brings its flare --
Stark in winter with bare, black limbs,
Delicately leaf'd out in early spring,

Full green, expansive, in summer skies,
And now, October, bravely sporting gold
Against the coming storm -- it speaks to me.

Whatever it produces from within
It gives away as freely as its leaves,
Trusting life to give them back again.

This perfect poem is rooted in the earth.
I stand a long time, listening.

THE NAMELESS

A cool, rainy morning in November,
Valley half hidden in fog,
The mountains in shredded clouds.

Ribbed contour of harrowed fields,
Aspens bare and blackened,
Animal tracks leading through tall grass.

Two miles down the gravel road, no one in sight,
I stop at the bottom of a drainage
Where stream plunges into thick bracken.

Smell of wet grass, soil and fallen leaves,
Specks of rain on my old vest,
Clouds tumbling heavy overhead.

Surrounds me here, huge, benevolent.
I tremble, like any tiny creature.

FIRST SNOW

It's cold tonight.
On the mountain ridge,
A rind of snow,
Like salt on the rim
Of a margarita glass.

The clouds hang low,
Portending the first storm --
Snow, blasts of wind,
Freezing cold.

Oh, bring it on --
Give it your best shot --
Sleet, hail, drifts five feet high --
We've waited all year
For this --

Bring it on.

RENAISSANCE

Miles from home, but not
Far enough to escape
The worries of the week,
Wound upon open wound,
The stain of human news
Smudging the heart,
I stop beside a drifted bank
To catch my breath,
Lean on the walking stick,
And look out over the meadow
Deep with softening snow,
And the tracks of one small animal
Striking out alone,
Across the windblown crust,
over the snowbridge covering the ravine,

Into the distant trees.

WINTER STARS

Tonight Orion
Raises his long leg
Over the mountain range,
Chasing the Pleiades,
Air frost clear
And stars like silver nails.

It is too cold to stay.
Old vest and black beret,
Head tilted back,
Shivering in short sleeves,
I blow out steamy air

And stare and stare.

THE GREAT SNOWBANK

Early April in the aspen grove,
Trees stand in wells of sunken snow.
On the windward slope, last winter's drift,
Huge, corniced, smudged by windblown chuff,
Shows each blizzard in its sculptured ribs.
It will remain, perhaps into late May,
Watering the meadow with its slow release.

The wet air smells of earth,
Ancient verities, reliable as spring,
The road softening and crimson spears
Piercing the gray mat of flat meadow grass.

My friend, the poet, is dying.
He will not see next winter's snow.
His poems bank the windward slope of sixty years
To nurture yet emerging generations.

A hawk lifts noiseless out of a bare tree,
Glides on wide wings over the broken fields,
                Searching . . .

THE MUSE

Not the spring freshets splashing noisily through
Fallen trees and big stones in the ravines.

Rather this rivulet, running like a ribbon
Of sky-blue silk through the spears of winter wheat.

BEFORE THE GODS

The road is closed to traffic by a gate.
I walk around it, follow the two rough ruts
Until they soften to a grassy path.

A deer trail leads up a rocky slope
Into scrub oak and mountain maples
With only a few leaves twittering on branches.

There is a white stone like a giant tooth
Thrusting five feet tall above the sagebrush.
My fingers brush its lichened skin.

Further, in an opening scattered with leaves,
Beneath a canopy of empty branches,
A small bird flitters in, sits without moving.

I take off my shoes,
Get down on my knees.
Bareheaded. Hands uplifted. Empty. Full.

ON PEBBLE ROAD

Ah, the perfect peace of being here,
After dark, the patio, a white armchair,
The crickets crocheting the cool night air,
And half moon lambent on the southern horizon,
Above the black shadow of the hayfield,
Silvering mountain ridges across the valley.

It is completely still and grand tonight.
The past seems weightless as a thistle seed,
The future, unfathomable as the stars.
I have arrived at last, after fifty-five years,
The heart at peace and free from all desire,
The mind as empty as the moonlit field,
Between two breaths, a moment without fear.

And oh, the perfect peace of being here.

FREE RANGE POET

Saturday morning,
With my walking stick,
No one waiting for me at home,
No schedule, no appointments,
No one who knows or cares
Where I am or when I will return,
I walk in my old clothes,
the road still frozen dirt,
The valley snowfields gleaming
And incandescence pouring between the peaks
In that sacred moment before sunrise.
I stride in perfect freedom,
Loosening my jacket,
Hearing only the crunch of my boots,
And the mad, jabbering birds,
Swinging my arms,
Clearing my head,
Singing pieces of old songs,
Kicking loose stones,
Up one steep hill
And down another,
Farther and farther,
I go on for hours,
Far beyond memory,
Deep beyond pain,
Into new country,
Farther and farther,
In perfect freedom,
I go as far as I can.

I ASK THE STARS TO BRING ME HOME AGAIN

Alone, outside, the night before I fly
  To some strange city half a world away,
I stand, head thrown back to the summer sky,
  The Milky Way spilled out like whale sperm,
And in the soft, southern sky, Saturn and Mars.

I am searching for the Perseid meteor shower,
  Heavenly fireworks, one hundred fifty an hour,
But find instead the fixed, immovable stars,
  The summer triangle -- Vega, Deneb, Altair --
A bracelet of valley lights reflecting the sky,
  And hayfields holding the dark house in their hands.

A satellite draws me into the Great Bear.
  This is where I want to live and die.

I ask the stars to bring me home again.

Photograph by Sierra Diane Wyndham, 2015

Harald Wyndham lives in Pocatello, Idaho where he publishes books under the Blue Scarab Press imprint. He recently retired after thirty-four years in the Semiconductor Industry. He and Jane have two grown children and three young adult grandchildren.

Thanks to the good people at Litho Printing -- Kelly, Kathy, Nathan and team -- for their efforts on behalf of this and the many prior Blue Scarab books.

And thanks to the community of Pocatello for supporting local writers, musicians and artists over the years.

OTHER BOOKS BY HARALD WYNDHAM

Rain Wakening, 1970

Epithalamion, 1971

Love & Marriage: A Sonnet Cycle, 1973

Down Home Ballads, by Chalmers Furgeson, 1974

From the Asylum, 1975

Pebble Creek, 1978; Confluence Press, Lewiston, Idaho

The Exile's Pilgrimage at Christmastide, 1979

Exile in a Cold Country, 1980

Cheap Mysteries: A Dimestore Decade of Poems, 1981

Strong in the Spirit, by Chalmers Furgeson, 1983

Homeland, 1984; Blue Scarab Press

Ohio Gothic, 1985; Blue Scarab Press

The Mount Moriah Studies, 1989; Blue Scarab Press

Kathedral, 1990; Blue Scarab Press

Prodigal Psalms, 1991; Blue Scarab Press

When You Love Me There Is One Universe, 1991

Heavenly Rhythm & Blues, Poems 1982 - 1993; Blue Scarab Press

The Four Seasons in Pocatello, 1995; Blue Scarab Press

The Christmas Sonnets, 1996; Blue Scarab Press

Tuscany, 2000; The Acid Press

The Little House of Poetry, Poems 1993 -2003; Blue Scarab Press

I Ask the Stars to Bring Me Home Again, 2008; Limberlost Press, Boise, Idaho

Sarajevo -- a poem for four voices in five parts, 2009; Blue Scarab Press

The Struggle, 2011; Blue Scarab Press

COLOPOHON

THE SAME MOON SHINES ON US ALL was type-set in Stone Serif and print-ed on Sundance Smooth text and Anthem Gloss cover in the fall of 2015, as fires afflicted many Western and Northwest states, reminding us with blood-red sunsets of the sacrifice made by valiant fire-fighters on our behalf.

Nonetheless, we count our blessings and remain stout of heart and bent on good cheer, despite the odds against humankind and all living things on this infinitesimal blue-green speck in the multiple universes of the cosmos.

May the same moon shine on us all.